1000 Ninja Foodi Air Fryer Cookbook with Pictures

Simple & Delicious Air Fry, Air Roast, Reheat, Dehydrate Food for Your Family & Friends
(for Beginners and Advanced Users)

Julia Adamo & Helen Bently

TABLE OF CONTENTS

Introduction

Ever since Ninja Foodi has stepped into the world of kitchen appliances, the company has introduced people to a range of multipurpose cooking appliances. Ninja Air fryer is one such example that has made waves of popularity due to its easy to use control panel and super-efficient Air frying mechanism. The device looks simple enough, yet it needs detailed guidance to tackle all sorts of troubleshooting situations. Every electric kitchen device should be used with care and smartness to enjoy a luscious meal every time. Here is why this cookbook offers a little guidance about the Ninja Air Fryer. Along with a set of scrumptious recipes, which are all created by experts using the Ninja Air Fryer.

What is Ninja Air fryer?

If you look at any model of the Ninja Air fryer, you would instantly recognize it due to its distinct shape, size, and exterior. Unlike multipurpose cookers, this Air fryer has a simple mechanism to cook. The entire unit consists of a base which contains all the heating system along with a space to insert the basket carrying food. It is this easy to use a system that makes the Air fryer ultra-smart and convenient for all of its users. All a person needs to do is to add food to the basket and insert the basket back in its place. Select the appropriate temperature and timing to cook the meal, and then the machine does the rest for you. Ninja Air fryer is available in four different models currently:

1. AF100
2. AF101
3. AF101C
4. AF101CCO

The AF100 does not come with a multilayer rack to accommodate food in two layers inside the cooking basket; the rest of the models are provided this rack, which makes cooking even more convenient. People assume that with every model, the size of the Fryer basket changes, which is hardly true because all of the models provide equal-sized base units and fryer baskets.

The Functions of Ninja Air Fryer

This Ninja Air fryer includes a ceramic crisper plate and a ceramic-coated basket. It has an Air Outlet Unit, main unit, a control panel, and air intake vent.

Ninja® Air Fryer Function

Air Fry: You can use this function to prepare crunchy and crispy food with little or no oil.

Air Roast: The roast unit prepares some tender meat and baked treats.

Reheat: Revive your leftover by warming it to crispy perfection.

Dehydrate: Now you can easily dehydrate the fruits and vegetables to prepare some easy snacks.

Operating Buttons

TEMP arrows you can up and down the temp arrows to adjust the cooking temperature.

TIME arrows: The time arrows are used to adjust the cooking time in any function.

START/PAUSE button: Once the time and temperature are selected for the specific recipe the **START/PAUSE** button starts cooking, pressing it again during the cooking stops the cooking process.

POWER button: The Power button shuts off the unit.

STANDBY MODE: After 10 minutes if no interaction is done with the control panel, the unit gets into a standby mode.

How to Use Ninja Air Fryer

The use of Ninja Foodi air fryer is easy as a touch of a button.

First, it is very crucial to grease the basket with oil spray.

You need to follow the recipe properly and do not overcrowd the basket.

You simply add the food to the basket and select the required function like AIR FRY, AIR roast, dehydrate or reheat.

Then adjust the cooking time and temperature using the operational buttons.

Once the food gets cooked, you can take out the basket and transfer the food to serving plates.

Maintaining and Cleaning the Appliance

- When using for the first time, discard all the packaging and wash the basket and other accessories that come with an air fryer.
- It is very important to read the inst appliance ructional manual.
- It is highly recommended to pay attention to all the warnings, operational instructions, tips, and safeguards to avoid damage or personal injury.
- It is not recommended to clean the main unit in the dishwasher.
- The accessories of the appliance are dishwasher safe and can be washed using the dishwasher.
- The Ninja air fryer is only intended to be used indoor.
- Remember to check the voltage indications are corresponding to the main voltage from the switch.
- It is not recommended to immerse the appliance in water.
- Keep the cord away from the reach of children and hot areas like stoves, heaters, etc.
- When operating, it's not recommended to touch the outer surface of the air fryer.
- Place the air fryer on a horizontal, sturdy, and flat surface.
- Unplug the appliance once done.
- Using any other accessory attachments that are not recommended by SharkNinja may cause electric shock, fire, or even injury.
- It is not recommended to use an air fryer for deep-frying with the oil.
- Make sure that the basket is closed before operating.
- Do not use a damaged cord or plugs to operate the appliance.
- Spilled food after cooking can cause serious burns, so wash the basket and clean the appliance after every use.

Cleaning of Air Fryer

- Let the appliance cool down properly before cleaning, then unplug the power cord of the air fryer.
- Make sure the appliance is properly cool down before cleaning.
- You can clean the outer surface by using a damp towel.
- Clean the inside of the air fryer with a nonabrasive sponge.
- The basket, crisper plate, and any other accessories can be easily washed in the dishwasher.
- Any food residue stuck to the basket can be cleaned by placing in the sink and filling it with soapy warm water for 5 minutes, then remove the residual with a soft sponge.

Breakfast Recipes

Pumpkin Muffins

Prep Time: 15 minutes.

Cook Time: 13 minutes.

Serves: 8

Ingredients:

- ½ cup pumpkin puree
- 1 cup gluten-free oats
- ¼ cup honey
- 1 medium egg beaten
- ½ teaspoon coconut butter
- ½ tablespoons cocoa nib
- ½ tablespoons vanilla essence
- Cooking spray
- ½ teaspoon nutmeg

Preparation:

1. At 375 degrees F, preheat your Air Fryer on Air fry mode.
2. Add oats, honey, eggs, pumpkin puree, coconut butter, cocoa nibs, vanilla essence, and nutmeg to a bowl and mix well until smooth.
3. Divide the batter into the muffin tray, greased with cooking spray.
4. Place the muffin tray in the Air Fryer Basket.
5. Return the Air Fryer Basket to the Air Fryer and cook for 13 minutes.
6. Initiate cooking by pressing the START/PAUSE BUTTON.
7. Allow the muffins to cool, then serve.

Serving Suggestion: Serve the muffins with hot coffee.

Variation Tip: Add raisins and nuts to the batter before baking.

Nutritional Information Per Serving:

Calories 209| Fat 7.5g|Sodium 321mg| Carbs 34.1g| Fiber 4g| Sugar 3.8g| Protein 4.3g

Air Fried Sausage

Prep Time: 10 minutes.

Cook Time: 13 minutes.

Serves: 4

Ingredients:

- 4 sausage links, raw and uncooked

Preparation:

1. At 390 degrees F, preheat your Air Fryer on Air fry mode.
2. Place the sausages in the Air Fryer Basket.
3. Return the Air Fryer Basket to the Air Fryer and cook for 13 minutes.
4. Initiate cooking by pressing the START/PAUSE BUTTON.
5. Serve warm and fresh.

Serving Suggestion: Serve the sausages with toasted bread and eggs.

Variation Tip: Add black pepper and salt for seasoning.

Nutritional Information Per Serving:
Calories 267| Fat 12g| Sodium 165mg| Carbs 39g| Fiber 1.4g| Sugar 22g| Protein 3.3g

Cinnamon Toasts

Prep Time: 15 minutes.
Cook Time: 8 minutes.
Serves: 4

Ingredients:
- 4 pieces of bread
- 2 tablespoons butter
- 2 eggs, beaten
- 1 pinch salt
- 1 pinch cinnamon ground
- 1 pinch nutmeg ground
- 1 pinch ground clove
- 1 teaspoon icing sugar

Preparation:
1. At 390 degrees F, preheat your Air Fryer on Air fry mode.
2. Add two eggs to a mixing bowl and stir cinnamon, nutmeg, ground cloves, and salt, then whisk well.

3. Spread butter on both sides of the bread slices and cut them into thick strips.
4. Dip the breadsticks in the egg mixture and place them in the Air Fryer Basket.
5. Return the Air Fryer Basket to the Air Fryer and cook for 8 minutes.

6. Initiate cooking by pressing the START/PAUSE BUTTON.
7. Flip the French toast sticks when cooked halfway through.
8. Serve.

Serving Suggestion: Serve the toasted with chocolate syrup or Nutella spread.

Variation Tip: Use crushed cornflakes for breading to have extra crispiness.

Nutritional Information Per Serving:

Calories 199| Fat 11.1g|Sodium 297mg| Carbs 14.9g| Fiber 1g| Sugar 2.5g| Protein 9.9g

Morning Egg Rolls

Prep Time: 15 minutes.

Cook Time: 13 minutes.

Serves: 6

Ingredients:

- 2 eggs
- 2 tablespoons milk
- Salt, to taste
- Black pepper, to taste
- 1/2 cup shredded cheddar cheese
- 2 sausage patties
- 6 egg roll wrappers
- 1 tablespoon olive oil
- 1 cup of water

Preparation:

1. At 375 degrees F, preheat your Air Fryer on Air fry mode.
2. Grease a small skillet with some olive oil and place it over medium heat.
3. Add sausage patties and cook them until brown.
4. Chop the cooked patties into small pieces. Beat eggs with salt, black pepper, and milk in a mixing bowl.
5. Grease the same skillet with 1 teaspoon olive oil and pour the egg mixture into it.
6. Stir cook to make scrambled eggs.
7. Add sausage, mix well and remove the skillet from the heat.
8. Spread an egg roll wrapper on the working surface in a diamond shape position.
9. Add a tablespoon of cheese at the bottom third of the roll wrapper.
10. Top the cheese with an egg mixture and wet the edges of the wrapper with water.
11. Fold the two corners of the wrapper and roll it, then seal the edges.
12. Repeat the same steps and place the rolls in the Air Fryer Basket.
13. Return the Air Fryer Basket to the Air Fryer and cook for 13 minutes.
14. Initiate cooking by pressing the START/PAUSE BUTTON.
15. Flip the rolls after 8 minutes and continue cooking for another 5 minutes.
16. Serve warm and fresh.

Serving Suggestion: Serve the rolls with your favorite hot sauce or cheese dip.

Variation Tip: Add crispy bacon to the filling.

Nutritional Information Per Serving:

Calories 282| Fat 15g| Sodium 526mg| Carbs 20g| Fiber 0.6g| Sugar 3.3g| Protein 16g

Spinach Egg Muffins

Prep Time: 10 minutes.

Cook Time: 13 minutes.

Serves: 4

Ingredients:

- 4 tablespoons milk
- 4 tablespoons frozen spinach, thawed
- 4 large egg
- 8 teaspoons grated cheese
- Salt, to taste
- Black pepper, to taste
- Cooking Spray

Preparation:

1. At 390 degrees F, preheat your Air Fryer on Air fry mode.
2. Grease four small-sized ramekin with cooking spray.
3. Add egg, cheese, spinach, and milk to a bowl and beat well.
4. Divide the mixture into the four small ramekins and top them with salt and black pepper.
5. Place the ramekins in the Air Fryer Basket.
6. Return the Air Fryer Basket to the Air Fryer and cook for 13 minutes.
7. Initiate cooking by pressing the START/PAUSE BUTTON.
8.   Serve warm.

Serving Suggestion: Serve the muffins with toasted bread slices and crispy bacon.

Variation Tip: Add sliced bell peppers to the muffins.

Nutritional Information Per Serving:

Calories 237| Fat 19g| Sodium 518mg| Carbs 7g| Fiber 1.5g| Sugar 3.4g| Protein 12g

Pepper Egg Cups

Prep Time: 15 minutes.

Cook Time: 18 minutes.

Serves: 4

Ingredients:

- 2 bell pepper, halved, seeds removed
- 4 eggs
- 1 teaspoon olive oil
- 1 pinch salt and black pepper
- 1 pinch sriracha flakes

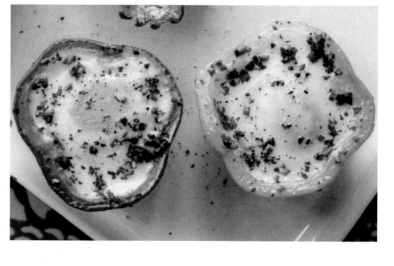

Preparation:

1. At 390 degrees F, preheat your Air Fryer on Air fry mode.
2. Slice the bell peppers in half, lengthwise, and remove their seeds and the inner portion to get a cup-like shape.
3. Rub olive oil on the edges of the bell peppers.
4. Place them in the Air Fryer Basket with their cut side up and crack 1 egg in each half of bell pepper.
5. Drizzle salt, black pepper, and sriracha flakes on top of the eggs.
6. Return the Air Fryer Basket to the Air Fryer and cook for 18 minutes.
7. Initiate cooking by pressing the START/PAUSE BUTTON.
8. Serve warm and fresh.

Serving Suggestion: Serve the cups with toasted bread slices and crispy bacon.

Variation Tip: Broil the cups with mozzarella cheese on top.

Nutritional Information Per Serving:

Calories 183| Fat 15g| Sodium 402mg| Carbs 2.5g| Fiber 0.4g| Sugar 1.1g| Protein 10g

Morning Patties

Prep Time: 15 minutes.

Cook Time: 13 minutes.

Serves: 4

Ingredients:

- 1 lb minced pork
- 1 lb minced turkey
- 2 teaspoons dry rubbed sage
- 2 teaspoons fennel seeds
- 2 teaspoons garlic powder
- 1 teaspoon paprika
- 1 teaspoon of sea salt

- 1 teaspoon dried thyme

Preparation:
1. At 390 degrees F, preheat your Air Fryer on Air fry mode.
2. In a mixing bowl, add turkey and pork, then mix them together.
3. Mix sage, fennel, paprika, salt, thyme, and garlic powder in a small bowl.
4. Drizzle this mixture over the meat mixture and mix well.
5. Take 2 tablespoons of this mixture at a time and roll it into thick patties.
6. Place the patties in the Air Fryer Basket, then spray them all with cooking oil.
7. Return the Air Fryer Basket to the Air Fryer and cook for 10 minutes.
8. Initiate cooking by pressing the START/PAUSE BUTTON.
9. Flip the patties in the basket once cooked halfway through.
10. Serve warm and fresh.

Serving Suggestion: Serve the patties with toasted bread slices.
Variation Tip: Ground chicken or beef can also be used instead of ground pork and turkey.
Nutritional Information Per Serving:
Calories 305| Fat 25g| Sodium 532mg| Carbs 2.3g| Fiber 0.4g| Sugar 2g| Protein 18.3g

Breakfast Bacon

Prep Time: 10 minutes.
Cook Time: 14 minutes.
Serves: 4
Ingredients:
- ½ lb of bacon slices

Preparation:

1. At 390 degrees F, preheat your Air Fryer on Air fry mode.
2. Spread the bacon slices in the Air Fryer Basket evenly in a single layer.
3. Return the Air Fryer Basket to the Air Fryer and cook for 14 minutes.
4. Initiate cooking by pressing the START/PAUSE BUTTON.
5. Flip the crispy bacon once cooked halfway through, then resume cooking.
6. Serve.

Serving Suggestion: Serve the bacon with eggs and bread slices
Variation Tip: Add salt and black pepper for seasoning.
Nutritional Information Per Serving:
Calories 273| Fat 22g| Sodium 517mg| Carbs 3.3g| Fiber 0.2g| Sugar 1.4g| Protein 16.1g

Crispy Hash Browns

Prep Time: 10 minutes.

Cook Time: 13 minutes.

Serves: 4

Ingredients:

- 3 russet potatoes
- ¼ cup chopped green peppers
- ¼ cup chopped red peppers
- ¼ cup chopped onions
- 2 garlic cloves chopped
- 1 teaspoon paprika
- Salt and black pepper, to taste
- 2 teaspoons olive oil

Preparation:

1. At 390 degrees F, preheat your Air Fryer on Air fry mode.
2. Peel and grate all the potatoes with the help of a cheese grater.
3. Add potato shreds to a bowl filled with cold water and leave it soaked for 25 minutes.
4. Drain the water and place the potato shreds on a plate lined with a paper towel.
5. Transfer the shreds to a dry bowl and add olive oil, paprika, garlic, and black pepper.
6. Make four flat patties out of the potato mixture and place them in the Air Fryer Basket.
7. Return the Air Fryer Basket to the Air Fryer and cook for 13 minutes.
8. Initiate cooking by pressing the START/PAUSE BUTTON.
9. Flip the potato hash browns once cooked halfway through, then resume cooking.
10. Once done, serve warm.

Serving Suggestion: Serve the hash with toasted bread slices and crispy bacon.

Variation Tip: Add herbed cream on top of the hash browns.

Nutritional Information Per Serving:

Calories 190| Fat 18g| Sodium 150mg| Carbs 0.6g| Fiber 0.4g| Sugar 0.4g| Protein 7.2g

Biscuit Balls

Prep Time: 10 minutes.

Cook Time: 18 minutes.

Serves: 6

Ingredients:

- 1 tablespoon butter
- 2 eggs, beaten
- ¼ teaspoons pepper
- 1 can (10.2 oz) Pillsbury Buttermilk biscuits
- 2 ounces cheddar cheese, diced into ten cubes
- Cooking spray
- Egg Wash
- 1 egg
- 1 tablespoon water

Preparation:

1. At 375 degrees F, preheat your Air Fryer on Air fry mode.
2. Place a suitable non-stick skillet over medium-high heat and cook the bacon until crispy, then place it on a plate lined with a paper towel.
3. Melt butter in the same skillet over medium heat. Beat eggs with pepper in a bowl and pour them into the skillet.
4. Stir cook for 5 minutes, then remove it from the heat.
5. Add bacon and mix well.
6. Divide the dough into 5 biscuits and slice each into 2 layers.
7. Press each biscuit into 4 inches round.
8. Add a tablespoon of the egg mixture at the center of each round and top it with a piece of cheese.
9. Carefully fold the biscuit dough around the filling and pinch the edges to seal.
10. Whisk egg with water in a small bowl and brush the egg wash over the biscuits.
11. Place the biscuit bombs in the Air Fryer Basket and spray them with cooking oil.
12. Return the Air Fryer Basket to the Air Fryer and cook for 14 minutes.
13. Initiate cooking by pressing the START/PAUSE BUTTON.
14. Flip the egg bombs when cooked halfway through, then resume cooking.
15. Serve warm

Serving Suggestion: Serve the eggs balls with crispy bacon.

Variation Tip: Add dried herbs to the egg filling.

Nutritional Information Per Serving:

Calories 102| Fat 7.6g| Sodium 545mg| Carbs 1.5g| Fiber 0.4g| Sugar 0.7g| Protein 7.1g

Snacks and Appetizers Recipes

Strawberries and Walnuts Muffins

Prep Time: 15 minutes.

Cook Time: 15 minutes.

Serves: 2

Ingredients

- Salt, pinch
- 2 eggs, whisked
- 1/3 cup maple syrup
- 1/3 cup coconut oil
- 4 tablespoons of water
- 1 teaspoon of orange zest
- ¼ teaspoon of vanilla extract
- ½ teaspoon of baking powder
- 1 cup all-purpose flour
- 1 cup strawberries, finely chopped
- 1/3 cup walnuts, chopped and roasted

Preparation:

1. Preheat the unit by selecting AIR FRY mode for 2 minutes at 325 degrees F.
2. Select START/PAUSE to begin the preheating process.
3. Once preheating is done, press START/PAUSE.
4. Take one cup size of 4 ramekins that are oven safe.
5. Layer it with muffin paper.
6. In a bowl and add egg, maple syrup, oil, water, vanilla extract, and orange zest.
7. Whisk it all very well
8. In a separate bowl, mix flour, baking powder, and salt.
9. Now add dry ingredients slowly to wet ingredients.
10. Now pour this batter into ramekins and top it with strawberries and walnuts.
11. Now put ramekins inside basket of air fryer and set the time to 15 minutes at 350 degrees F.
12. Check if not done let it AIR FRY for one more minute.
13. Once done, serve.

Serving Suggestion: serve it with coffee

Variation Tip: use vegetable oil instead of coconut oil

Nutritional Information Per Serving:

Calories 897| Fat 53.9g| Sodium 148mg| Carbs 92g| Fiber 4.7g| Sugar35.6g| Protein 17.5g

Stuffed Bell Peppers

Prep Time: 25 minutes.

Cook Time: 16 minutes.

Serves: 3

Ingredients:

- 6 large bell peppers
- 1-1/2 cup cooked rice
- 2 cups cheddar cheese

Preparation:

1. Preheat the unit by selecting AIR FRY mode for 5 minutes at 350 degrees F.
2. Select START/PAUSE to begin the preheating process.
3. Once preheating is done, press START/PAUSE.
4. Cut the bell peppers in half lengthwise and remove all the seeds.
5. Fill the cavity of each bell pepper with cooked rice.
6. Grease the basket of air fryer with oil spray
7. Transfer the bell peppers to the basket of the Ninja air fryer.
8. Set the time for 200 degrees for 10 minutes.
9. Afterward, take out the basket and sprinkle cheese on top.
10. Set the time at 200 degrees for 6 minutes.
11. Once it's done, serve.

Serving Suggestion: Serve it with mashed potato

Variation Tip: You can use any cheese you like

Nutritional Information Per Serving:

Calories 605| Fat 26g| Sodium 477mg| Carbs 68.3g| Fiber 4g| Sugar 12.5g| Protein 25.6g

Spicy Chicken Tenders

Prep Time: 15 minutes.

Cook Time: 12 minutes.

Serves: 2

Ingredients:

- 2 large eggs, whisked
- 2 tablespoons lemon juice

- Salt and black pepper
- 1 pound of chicken tenders
- 1 cup Panko breadcrumbs
- 1/2 cup Italian bread crumb
- 1 teaspoon smoked paprika
- 1/4 teaspoon garlic powder
- 1/4 teaspoon onion powder
- 1/2 cup fresh grated parmesan cheese

Preparation:

1. Preheat the unit by selecting AIR FRY mode for 2 minutes at 325 degrees F.
2. Select START/PAUSE to begin the preheating process.
3. Once preheating is done, press START/PAUSE.
4. Take a bowl and whisk eggs in it and set aside for further use.
5. In a large bowl add lemon juice, paprika, salt, black pepper, garlic powder, onion powder
6. In a separate bowl mix Panko breadcrumbs, Italian bread crumbs, and parmesan cheese.
7. Dip the chicken tenders in the spice mixture and coat the entire tender well.
8. Let the tenders sit for 1 hour.
9. Then dip each chicken tender in egg and then in bread crumbs.
10. Line the basket of the air fryer with parchment paper.
11. Transfer the tenders to the basket.
12. Set it to air fry mode at 350 degrees F for 12 minutes.
13. Once it's done, serve.

Serving Suggestion: Serve it with ketchup

Variation Tip: Use mild paprika instead of smoked paprika

Nutritional Information Per Serving:

Calories 836| Fat 36g| Sodium 1307mg| Carbs 31.3g| Fiber 2.5g| Sugar 3.3 g| Protein 95.3g

Sweet Bites

Prep Time: 25 minutes.
Cook Time: 10 minutes.
Serves: 4

Ingredients:

- 10 sheets of Phyllo dough, (filo dough)
- 2 tablespoons of melted butter
- 1 cup walnuts, chopped

- 2 teaspoons of honey
- Pinch of cinnamon
- 1 teaspoon of orange zest

Preparation:

1. Preheat the unit by selecting AIR FRY mode for 2 minutes at 325 degrees F.
2. Select START/PAUSE to begin the preheating process.
3. Once preheating is done, press START/PAUSE.
4. First, layer together 10 Phyllo dough sheets on a flat surface.
5. Then cut it into 4 *4-inch squares.
6. Now, coat the squares with butter, drizzle some honey, orange zest, walnuts, and cinnamon.
7. Bring all 4 corners together and press the corners to make a little like purse design.
8. Put it inside the air fryer basket and select the AIR fry mode and set it for 10 minutes at 375 degrees F.
9. Once done, take out and serve.

Serving Suggestion: Serve with a topping of nuts

Variation Tip: None

Nutritional Information Per Serving:

Calories 397| Fat 27.1g| Sodium 271mg| Carbs 31.2g| Fiber 3.2g| Sugar3.3g| Protein 11g

Parmesan Crush Chicken

Prep Time: 20 minutes.

Cook Time: 18 minutes.

Serves: 4

Ingredients:

- 4 chicken breasts
- 1 cup parmesan cheese
- 1 cup bread crumb
- 2 eggs, whisked
- Salt, to taste
- Oil spray, for greasing

Preparation:

1. Preheat the unit by selecting AIR FRY mode for 5 minutes at 325 degrees F.
2. Select START/PAUSE to begin the preheating process.
3. Once preheating is done, press START/PAUSE.
4. Whisk egg in a large bowl and set aside.
5. Season the chicken breast with salt and then put it in egg wash.
6. Next, dredge it in breadcrumb then parmesan cheese.
7. Line the basket of the air fryer with parchment paper.
8. Put the breast pieces inside the basket, and oil spray the breast pieces.

9. Set it to air fry mode at 350 degrees F, for 18 minutes.

10. Once it's done, serve.

Serving Suggestion: Serve it with ketchup

Variation Tip: Use cheddar cheese instead of parmesan

Nutritional Information Per Serving:

Calories 574| Fat 25g| Sodium 848mg| Carbs 21.4g| Fiber 1.2g| Sugar 1.8g| Protein 64.4g

Dijon Cheese Sandwich

Prep Time: 10 minutes.

Cook Time: 10 minutes.

Serves: 2

Ingredients:

- 4 large slices sourdough, whole grain
- 4 tablespoons of Dijon mustard
- 1-1/2 cup grated sharp cheddar cheese
- 2 teaspoons green onion, chopped the green part
- 2 tablespoons of butter melted

Preparation:

1. Preheat the unit by selecting AIR FRY mode for 2 minutes at 325 degrees F.
2. Select START/PAUSE to begin the preheating process.
3. Once preheating is done, press START/PAUSE.
4. Brush the melted butter on one side of all the bread slices.
5. Then spread Dijon mustard on other sides of slices.
6. Then top the 2 bread slices with cheddar cheese and top it with green onions.
7. Cover with the remaining two slices to make two sandwiches.
8. Put it to the basket of the air fryer.
9. Turn on the air fry mode at 350 degrees f, for 10 minutes.
10. Once it's done, serve.

Serving Suggestion: Serve with tomato soup

Variation Tip: Use oil spray instead of butter

Nutritional Information Per Serving:

Calories 617| fat 38g| sodium 1213mg| carbs 40.8g| fiber 5g| sugar 5.6g| protein 29.5g

Cheddar Quiche

Prep Time: 10 minutes.

Cook Time: 12 minutes.

Serves: 2

Ingredients:

- 4 eggs, organic
- 1-1/4 cup heavy cream
- Salt, pinch
- ½ cup broccoli florets
- ½ cup cheddar cheese, shredded and for sprinkling

Preparation:
1. Take a Pyrex pitcher and crack two eggs in it.
2. And fill it with heavy cream, about half the way up.
3. Add in the salt and then add in the broccoli and pour this into a quiche dish, and top it with shredded cheddar cheese.
4. Preheat the unit by selecting AIR FRY mode for 2 minutes at 325 degrees F.
5. Select START/PAUSE to begin the preheating process.
6. Once preheating is done, press START/PAUSE.
7. Now put the dish inside air fryer basket.
8. Set the time to 12 minutes at 325 degrees F.
9. Once done, serve hot.

Serving Suggestion: Serve with herbs as a topping
Variation Tip: Use spinach instead of broccoli florets
Nutritional Information Per Serving:
Calories 454| Fat 40g| Sodium 406mg| Carbs 4.2g| Fiber 0.6g| Sugar 1.3g| Protein 20g

Grill Cheese Sandwich

Prep Time: 15 minutes.
Cook Time: 10 minutes.
Serves: 2

Ingredients:
- 4 slices of white bread slices
- 2 tablespoons of butter, melted
- 2 slices of sharp cheddar
- 2 slices of Swiss cheese
- 2 slices of mozzarella cheese

Preparation:
1. Preheat the unit by selecting AIR FRY mode for 2 minutes at 325 degrees F.

2. Select START/PAUSE to begin the preheating process.
3. Once preheating is done, press START/PAUSE.
4. Brush melted butter on one side of all the bread slices and then top the 2 bread slices with slices of cheddar, Swiss, and mozzarella, one slice per bread.
5. Top it with the other slice to make a sandwich.
6. Add it to the basket of the air fryer.
7. Turn on AIR FRY mode at 350 degrees F for 10 minutes.
8. Once done, serve.

Serving Suggestion: Serve with tomato soup
Variation Tip: Use oil spray instead of butter
Nutritional Information Per Serving:
Calories 577| Fat 38g| Sodium 1466mg| Carbs 30.5g| Fiber 1.1g| Sugar 6.5g| Protein 27.6g

Blueberries Muffins

Prep Time: 15 minutes.
Cook Time: 15 minutes.
Serves: 2
Ingredients:
- Salt, pinch
- 2 eggs
- 1/3 cup sugar
- 1/3 cup vegetable oil
- 4 tablespoons of water
- 1 teaspoon of lemon zest
- ¼ teaspoon of vanilla extract
- ½ teaspoon of baking powder
- 1 cup all-purpose flour
- 1 cup blueberries

Preparation:
1. Take 4 one-cup sized ramekins that are oven safe and layer them with muffin papers.
2. Take a bowl and whisk the egg, sugar, oil, water, vanilla extract, and lemon zest.
3. Whisk it all very well.
4. Now, in a separate bowl, mix the flour, baking powder, and salt.
5. Now, add dry ingredients slowly to wet ingredients.
6. Now, pour this batter into ramekins and top it with blueberries.
7. Preheat the unit by selecting AIR FRY mode for 2 minutes at 325 degrees F.
8. Select START/PAUSE to begin the preheating process.
9. Once preheating is done, press START/PAUSE.
10. Now, place the ramekins inside the Ninja Foodi Air Fryer.

11. Set the time to AIRFRY mode for 15 minutes at 350 degrees F.

12. Check if not done, and let it AIR FRY for one more minute.

13. Once it is done, serve.

Serving Suggestion: Serve it with whipped cream topping

Variation Tip: use butter instead of vegetable oil

Nutritional Information Per Serving:

Calories 781| Fat 41.6g| Sodium 143mg| Carbs 92.7g| Fiber 3.5g| Sugar 41.2g| Protein 0g

Chicken Tenders

Prep Time: 15 minutes.

Cook Time: 12 minutes.

Serves: 3

Ingredients:

- 1 pound of chicken tender
- Salt and black pepper, to taste
- 1 cup Panko bread crumbs
- 2 cups Italian bread crumbs
- 1 cup parmesan cheese
- 2 eggs
- Oil spray, for greasing

Preparation:

1. Sprinkle the tenders with salt and black pepper.

2. In a medium bowl mix Panko bread crumbs with Italian breadcrumbs.

3. Add salt, pepper, and parmesan cheese.

4. Crack two eggs in a bowl.

5. First, put the chicken tender in eggs.

6. Now dredge the tender in a bowl and coat the tender well with crumbs.

7. Preheat the unit by selecting AIR FRY mode for 2 minutes at 325 degrees F.

8. Select START/PAUSE to begin the preheating process.

9. Once preheating is done, press START/PAUSE.

10. Line the basket of the air fryer with parchment paper.

11. At the end spray the tenders with oil spray.

12. Layer the tenders inside the basket of Ninja Foodi Air Fryer.

13. Set it to the AIR FRY mode at 350 degrees F for 12 minutes.

14. Once it's done, serve.

Serving Suggestion: Serve it with ranch or ketchup

Variation Tip: Use Italian seasoning instead of Italian bread crumbs

Nutritional Information Per Serving:

Calories 558| Fat 23.8g| Sodium 872mg| Carbs 20.9g| Fiber 1.7g| Sugar 2.2g| Protein 63.5g

Vegetables and Sides Recipes

Curly Fries

Prep Time: 10 minutes.

Cook Time: 20 minutes.

Serves: 6

Ingredients:

- 2 Spiralized Zucchinis
- 1 cup flour
- 2 tbs paprika
- 1 teaspoon cayenne pepper
- 1 teaspoon garlic powder
- 1 teaspoon black pepper
- 1 teaspoon salt
- 2 eggs
- olive oil or cooking spray

Preparation:

1. At 390 degrees F, preheat your Air Fryer on Air fry mode.
2. Mix flour with paprika, cayenne pepper, garlic powder, black pepper, and salt in a bowl.
3. Beat eggs in another bowl and dip the zucchini in the eggs.
4. Coat the zucchini with the flour mixture and place into the Air Fryer Basket.
5. Spray the zucchini with cooking oil.
6. Return the Air Fryer Basket to the Air Fryer and cook for 20 minutes.
7. Initiate cooking by pressing the START/PAUSE BUTTON.
8. Toss the zucchini once cooked halfway through, then resume cooking.
9. Serve warm.

Serving Suggestion: Serve with red chunky salsa or chili sauce.

Variation Tip: Use crushed cornflakes for breading to have extra crispiness.

Nutritional Information Per Serving:

Calories 212| Fat 11.8g| Sodium 321mg| Carbs 24.6g| Fiber 4.4g| Sugar 8g| Protein 7.3g

Saucy Carrots

Prep Time: 15 minutes.

Cook Time: 25 minutes.

Serves: 6

Ingredients:

- 1 lb. cup carrots, cut into chunks

- 1 tablespoon sesame oil
- ½ tablespoons ginger, minced
- ½ tablespoons soy sauce
- ½ teaspoon garlic, minced
- ½ tablespoons scallions, chopped, for garnish
- ½ teaspoon sesame seeds for garnish

Preparation:

1. At 390 degrees F, preheat your Air Fryer on Air fry mode.
2. Toss all the ginger carrots ingredients, except the sesame seeds and scallions, in a suitable bowl.
3. Place the carrots in the Air Fryer Basket in a single layer.
4. Return the Air Fryer Basket to the Air Fryer and cook for 25 minutes.
5. Initiate cooking by pressing the START/PAUSE BUTTON.
6. Toss the carrots once cooked halfway through.
7. Garnish with sesame seeds and scallions.
8. Serve warm

Serving Suggestion: Serve with mayo sauce or ketchup.

Variation Tip: Use some honey for a sweet taste.

Nutritional Information Per Serving:

Calories 206| Fat 3.4g| Sodium 174mg| Carbs 35g| Fiber 9.4g| Sugar 5.9g| Protein 10.6g

Fried Artichoke Hearts

Prep Time: 15 minutes.

Cook Time: 10 minutes.

Serves: 6

Ingredients:

- 3 cans Quartered Artichokes, drained
- 1/2 cup mayonnaise
- 1 cup panko breadcrumbs
- ⅓ cup grated Parmesan
- salt and black pepper to taste
- Parsley for garnish

Preparation:

1. At 375 degrees F, preheat your Air Fryer on Air fry mode.
2. Mix mayonnaise with salt and black pepper and keep the sauce aside.
3. Spread panko breadcrumbs in a bowl.

4. Coat the artichoke pieces with the breadcrumbs.

5. As you coat the artichokes, place them in the Air Fryer Basket in a single layer, then spray them with cooking oil.

6. Return the Air Fryer Basket to the Air Fryer and cook for 10 minutes.

7. Initiate cooking by pressing the START/PAUSE BUTTON.

8. Flip the artichokes once cooked halfway through, then resume cooking.

9. Serve warm with mayo sauce.

Serving Suggestion: Serve with red chunky salsa or chili sauce.

Variation Tip: Use crushed cornflakes for breading to have extra crispiness.

Nutritional Information Per Serving:

Calories 193 | Fat 1g |Sodium 395mg | Carbs 38.7g | Fiber 1.6g | Sugar 0.9g | Protein 6.6g

Fried Olives

Prep Time: 15 minutes.

Cook Time: 9 minutes.

Serves: 6

Ingredients:

- 2 cups blue cheese stuffed olives, drained
- 1/2 cup all-purpose flour
- 1 cup panko breadcrumbs
- 1/2 teaspoons garlic powder
- 1 pinch of oregano
- 2 eggs

Preparation:

1. At 375 degrees F, preheat your Air Fryer on Air fry mode.

2. Mix flour with oregano and garlic powder in a bowl and beat two eggs in another bowl.

3. Spread panko breadcrumbs in a bowl.

4. Coat all the olives with the flour mixture, dip in the eggs and then coat with the panko breadcrumbs.

5. As you coat the olives, place them in the Air Fryer Basket in a single layer, then spray them with cooking oil.

6. Return the Air Fryer Basket to the Air Fryer and cook for 9 minutes.

7. Initiate cooking by pressing the START/PAUSE BUTTON.

8. Flip the olives once cooked halfway through, then resume cooking.

9. Serve.

Serving Suggestion: Serve with red chunky salsa or chili sauce.

Variation Tip: Use crushed cornflakes for breading to have extra crispiness.

Nutritional Information Per Serving:

Calories 166| Fat 3.2g| Sodium 437mg| Carbs 28.8g| Fiber 1.8g| Sugar 2.7g| Protein 5.8g

Falafel

Prep Time: 15 minutes.

Cook Time: 14 minutes.

Serves: 6

Ingredients:

- 1 (15.5 oz) can chickpeas, rinsed and drained
- 1 small yellow onion, cut into quarters
- 3 garlic cloves, chopped
- 1/3 cup parsley, chopped
- 1/3 cup cilantro, chopped
- 1/3 cup scallions, chopped
- 1 teaspoon cumin
- 1/2 teaspoons salt
- 1/8 teaspoons crushed red pepper flakes
- 1 teaspoon baking powder
- 4 tablespoons all-purpose flour
- Olive oil spray

Preparation:

1. At 350 degrees F, preheat your Air Fryer on Air fry mode.
2. Dry the chickpeas on paper towels.
3. Add onions and garlic to a food processor and chop them.
4. Add the parsley, salt, cilantro, scallions, cumin, and red pepper flakes.
5. Press the pulse button for 60 seconds, then toss in chickpeas and blend for 3 times until it makes a chunky paste.
6. Stir in baking powder and flour and mix well.
7. Transfer the falafel mixture to a bowl and cover to refrigerate for 3 hours.
8. Make 12 balls out of the falafel mixture.
9. Place falafels in the Air Fryer Basket and spray them with oil.
10. Return the Air Fryer Basket to the Air Fryer and cook for 14 minutes.
11. Initiate cooking by pressing the START/PAUSE BUTTON.
12. Toss the falafel once cooked halfway through, and resume cooking.
13. Serve warm

Serving Suggestion: Serve with yogurt dip and sautéed carrots.

Variation Tip: Use breadcrumbs for breading to have extra crispiness.

Nutritional Information Per Serving:

Calories 113| Fat 3g| Sodium 152mg| Carbs 20g| Fiber 3g| Sugar 1.1g| Protein 3.5g

Quinoa Patties

Prep Time: 15 minutes.
Cook Time: 32 minutes.
Serves: 4

Ingredients:
- 1 cup quinoa red
- 1½ cups water
- 1 teaspoon salt
- black pepper, ground
- 1½ cups rolled oats
- 3 eggs beaten
- ¼ cup minced white onion
- ½ cup crumbled feta cheese
- ¼ cup chopped fresh chives
- Salt and black pepper, to taste
- Vegetable or canola oil

Cucumber yogurt dill sauce
- 1 cup cucumber, diced
- 1 cup Greek yogurt
- 2 teaspoons lemon juice
- ¼ teaspoons salt

- 4 hamburger buns
- 4 arugulas
- 4 slices tomato sliced

- Black pepper, ground
- 1 tablespoon chopped fresh dill
- 1 tablespoon olive oil

Preparation:
1. At 390 degrees F, preheat your Air Fryer on Air fry mode.
2. Add quinoa to a saucepan filled with cold water, salt, and black pepper, and place it over medium-high heat.
3. Cook the quinoa to a boil, then reduce the heat, cover, and cook for 20 minutes on a simmer.
4. Fluff and mix the cooked quinoa with a fork and remove it from the heat.
5. Spread the quinoa in a baking stay.
6. Mix eggs, oats, onion, herbs, cheese, salt, and black pepper.
7. Stir in quinoa, then mix well. Make 4 patties out of this quinoa cheese mixture.
8. Place the patties in the Air Fryer Basket and spray them with cooking oil.
9. Return the Air Fryer Basket to the Air Fryer and cook for 13 minutes.
10. Initiate cooking by pressing the START/PAUSE BUTTON.
11. Flip the patties once cooked halfway through, and resume cooking.
12. Meanwhile, prepare the cucumber yogurt dill sauce by mixing all of its ingredients in a mixing bowl.
13. Place each quinoa patty in a burger bun along with arugula leaves.
14. Serve with yogurt dill sauce.

Serving Suggestion: Serve with yogurt dip.
Variation Tip: Use crushed cornflakes for breading to have extra crispiness.
Nutritional Information Per Serving:
Calories 231| Fat 9g| Sodium 271mg| Carbs 32.8g| Fiber 6.4g| Sugar 7g | Protein 6.3g

Lime Glazed Tofu

Prep Time: 10 minutes.

Cook Time: 14 minutes.

Serves: 6

Ingredients:

- ⅔ cup coconut amines
- 2 (14 oz) packages extra-firm, water-packed tofu, drained
- 6 tablespoons toasted sesame oil
- ⅔ cup lime juice

Preparation:

1. At 400 degrees F, preheat your Air Fryer on Air fry mode.
2. Pat dry the tofu bars and slice into half-inch cubes.
3. Toss all the remaining ingredients in a small bowl.
4. Marinate for 4 hours in the refrigerator. Drain off the excess water.
5. Place the tofu cubes in the Air Fryer Basket.
6. Return the Air Fryer Basket to the Air Fryer and cook for 14 minutes.
7. Initiate cooking by pressing the START/PAUSE BUTTON.
8. Toss the tofu once cooked halfway through, then resume cooking.
9. Serve warm

Serving Suggestion: Serve with sautéed green vegetables.

Variation Tip: Add sautéed onion and carrot to the tofu cubes.

Nutritional Information Per Serving:

Calories 284| Fat 7.9g| Sodium 704mg| Carbs 38.1g| Fiber 1.9g| Sugar 1.9g| Protein 14.8g

Sweet Potatoes with Honey Butter

Prep Time: 15 minutes.

Cook Time: 40 minutes.

Serves: 4

Ingredients:

- 4 sweet potatoes, scrubbed
- 1 teaspoon oil

Honey Butter

- 4 tablespoons unsalted butter
- 1 tablespoon Honey
- 2 teaspoons hot sauce
- ¼ teaspoons salt

Preparation:

1. At 390 degrees F, preheat your Air Fryer on Air fry mode.
2. Rub the sweet potatoes with oil and place two potatoes in the Air Fryer Basket.
3. Return the Air Fryer Basket to the Air Fryer and cook for 40 minutes.
4. Initiate cooking by pressing the START/PAUSE BUTTON.
5. Flip the potatoes once cooked halfway through, then resume cooking.
6. Mix butter with hot sauce, honey, and salt in a bowl.
7. When the potatoes are done, cut a slit on top and make a well with a spoon
8. Pour the honey butter into each potato jacket.
9. Serve.

Serving Suggestion: Serve with sautéed vegetables and salad.

Variation Tip: Sprinkle crumbled bacon and parsley on top.

Nutritional Information Per Serving:

Calories 288| Fat 6.9g| Sodium 761mg| Carbs 46g| Fiber 4g| Sugar 12g| Protein 9.6g

Hasselback Potatoes

Prep Time: 15 minutes.

Cook Time: 15 minutes.

Serves: 4

Ingredients:

- 4 medium Yukon Gold potatoes
- 3 tablespoons melted butter
- 1 tablespoon olive oil
- 3 garlic cloves, crushed
- ½ teaspoon ground paprika
- Salt and black pepper ground, to taste
- 1 tablespoon chopped fresh parsley

Preparation:

1. At 375 degrees F, preheat your Air Fryer on Air fry mode.
2. Slice each potato from the top to make 1/4-inch slices without cutting its 1/2-inch bottom, keeping the potato's bottom intact.
3. Mix butter with olive oil, garlic, and paprika in a small bowl.
4. Brush the garlic mixture on top of each potato and add the mixture into the slits.
5. Season them with salt and black pepper.
6. Place the seasoned potatoes in the Air Fryer Basket
7. Return the Air Fryer Basket to the Air Fryer and cook for 25 minutes.
8. Initiate cooking by pressing the START/PAUSE BUTTON.
9. Brushing the potatoes again with butter mixture after 15 minutes, then resume cooking.
10. Garnish with parsley.

11. Serve warm

Serving Suggestion: Serve with mayonnaise or cream cheese dip.

Variation Tip: Add tomato and cheese slices to the potato slits before air frying.

Nutritional Information Per Serving:

Calories 350| Fat 2.6g|Sodium 358mg| Carbs 64.6g| Fiber 14.4g| Sugar 3.3g| Protein 19.9g

Zucchini Cakes

Prep Time: 10 minutes.

Cook Time: 32 minutes.

Serves: 6

Ingredients:
- 2 medium zucchinis, grated
- 1 cup corn kernel
- 1 medium potato cooked
- 2 tablespoons chickpea flour
- 2 garlic minced
- 2 teaspoons olive oil
- Salt and black pepper
- For Serving:
- Yogurt tahini sauce

Preparation:

1. At 390 degrees F, preheat your Air Fryer on Air fry mode.
2. Mix grated zucchini with a pinch of salt in a colander and leave them for 15 minutes.
3. Squeeze out their excess water.
4. Mash the cooked potato in a large-sized bowl with a fork.
5. Add zucchini, corn, garlic, chickpea flour, salt, and black pepper to the bowl.
6. Mix these fritters' ingredients together and make 2 tablespoons-sized balls out of this mixture and flatten them lightly.
7. Place the fritters in the Air Fryer Basket in a single layer and spray them with cooking.
8. Return the Air Fryer Basket to the Air Fryer and cook for 17 minutes.
9. Initiate cooking by pressing the START/PAUSE BUTTON.
10. Flip the fritters once cooked halfway through, then resume cooking.
11. Serve

Serving Suggestion: Serve with mayonnaise or cream cheese dip.

Variation Tip: Use crushed cornflakes for breading to have extra crispiness.

Nutritional Information Per Serving:

Calories 270| Fat 14.6g| Sodium 394mg| Carbs 31.3g| Fiber 7.5g| Sugar 9.7g| Protein 6.4g

Air Fried Okra

Prep Time: 10 minutes.

Cook Time: 13 minutes.

Serves: 2

Ingredients:

- ½ lb okra pods sliced
- 1 teaspoon olive oil
- ¼ teaspoons salt
- ⅛ teaspoons black pepper

Preparation:

1. At 375 degrees F, preheat your Air Fryer on Air fry mode.
2. Toss okra with olive oil, salt, and black pepper in a bowl.
3. Spread the okra in a single layer in the Air Fryer Basket.
4. Return the Air Fryer Basket to the Air Fryer and cook for 13 minutes.
5. Initiate cooking by pressing the START/PAUSE BUTTON.
6. Toss the okra once cooked halfway through, and resume cooking.
7. Serve warm

Serving Suggestion: Serve with potato chips and bread slices.

Variation Tip: Sprinkle cornmeal before cooking for added crispiness.

Nutritional Information Per Serving:

Calories 208| Fat 5g| Sodium 1205mg| Carbs 34.1g| Fiber 7.8g| Sugar 2.5g| Protein 5.9g

Beef, Lamb and Pork Recipes

Ham Burger Patties

Prep Time: 15 minutes.

Cook Time: 16 minutes.

Serves: 2

Ingredients:

- 1 pound of ground beef
- Salt and pepper, to taste
- ½ teaspoon of red chili powder
- ¼ teaspoon of coriander powder
- 2 tablespoons of chopped onion
- 1 green chili, chopped
- Oil spray for greasing
- 2 large potato wedges

Preparation:

1. Take out the rack and oil greases the air fryer basket with oil spray.

2. Add potato wedges in the basket.

3. Put the rack on top and cover it with aluminum foil.

4. Take a bowl and add minced beef in it and add salt, pepper, chili powder, coriander powder, green chili, and chopped onion.

5. Mix well and make two burger patties with wet hands.

6. Put the patties beside wedges inside air fryer.

7. Now, set time for 12 minutes using AIR FRY mode at 400 degrees F.

8. Once the time of cooking complete, take out the basket.

9. Flip the patties and turn and twist the potatoes wedges.

10. Again, set time for 4 minutes at 400 degrees F

11. Once it's done, serve and enjoy.

Serving Suggestion: Serve it with bread slices, cheese, and pickles, lettuce, and onion

Variation Tip: None

Nutritional Information Per Serving:

Calories 875| Fat 21.5g| Sodium 622mg| Carbs 88g| Fiber10.9 g| Sugar 3.4g| Protein 78.8g

Bell Peppers with Sausages

Prep Time: 15 minutes.

Cook Time: 15 minutes.

Serves: 4

Ingredients:

- 6 beef or pork Italian sausages
- 4 bell peppers, whole
- Oil spray, for greasing
- 2 cups of cooked rice
- 1 cup of sour cream

Preparation:

1. Preheat the unit by selecting AIR FRY mode for 2 minutes at 325 degrees F.
2. Select START/PAUSE to begin the preheating process.
3. Once preheating is done, press START/PAUSE.
4. Put the bell pepper inside the basket and sausages accommodating aside.
5. Now, place the basket inside the unit.
6. Set it to AIR FRY MODE for 15 minutes at 400 degrees F.
7. Once done and serve over cooked rice with a dollop of sour cream.

Serving Suggestion: Serve it with salad

Variation Tip: use olive oil instead of oil spray.

Nutritional Information Per Serving:

Calories 1356| Fat 81.2g| Sodium 3044 mg| Carbs 96g| Fiber 3.1g| Sugar 8.3g| Protein 57.2 g

Pork Chops

Prep Time: 10 minutes.

Cook Time: 20 minutes.

Serves: 2

Ingredients:

- 1 tablespoon of rosemary, chopped
- Salt and black pepper, to taste
- 2 garlic cloves
- 1-inch ginger
- 2 tablespoons of olive oil
- 8 pork chops

Preparation:

1. Take a blender and pulse together rosemary, salt, pepper, garlic cloves, ginger, and olive oil.
2. Rub this marinade over pork chops and let it rest for 1 hour.

3. Then adjust it inside the air fryer and set it to AIR FRY mode for 20 minutes at 375 degrees F.

4. Once the cooking cycle is done, take out and serve hot.

Serving Suggestion: Serve it with salad

Variation Tip: Use canola oil instead of olive oil

Nutritional Information Per Serving:

Calories 1154| Fat 93.8g| Sodium 225mg| Carbs 2.1g| Fiber 0.8g| Sugar 0g| Protein 72.2g

Spicy Lamb Chops

Prep Time: 15 minutes.

Cook Time: 15 minutes.

Serves: 4

Ingredients:

- 12 lamb chops, bone-in
- Salt and black pepper, to taste
- ½ teaspoon of lemon zest
- 1 tablespoon of lemon juice
- 1 teaspoon of paprika
- 1 teaspoon of garlic powder
- ½ teaspoon of Italian seasoning
- ¼ teaspoon of onion powder

Preparation:

1. Preheat the unit by selecting AIR FRY mode for 2 minutes at 325 degrees F.

2. Select START/PAUSE to begin the preheating process.

3. Once preheating is done, press START/PAUSE.

4. Add the lamb chops to the bowl and sprinkle salt, garlic powder, Italian seasoning, onion powder, black pepper, lemon zest, lemon juice, and paprika.

5. Rub the chops well, and transfer it to the basket of the air fryer.

6. Set the air fryer at 400 degrees F, for 15 minutes at AIR FRY mode.

7. After 10 minutes, take out the basket and flip the chops.

8. Cook for the remaining minutes, and then serve.

Serving Suggestion: Serve it over rice

Variation Tip: None

Nutritional Information Per Serving:

Calories 787| Fat 45.3g| Sodium 1mg| Carbs 16.1g| Fiber 0.3g| Sugar 0.4g| Protein 75.3g

Short Ribs & Root Vegetables

Prep Time: 15 minutes.

Cook Time: 45 minutes.

Serves: 2

Ingredients:

- 1 pound of beef short ribs, bone-in and trimmed
- Salt and black pepper, to taste
- 2 tablespoons canola oil, divided
- 1/4 cup red wine
- 3 tablespoons brown sugar
- 2 cloves garlic, peeled, minced
- 4 carrots, peeled, cut into 1-inch pieces
- 2 parsnips, peeled, cut into 1-inch pieces
- ½ cup pearl onions

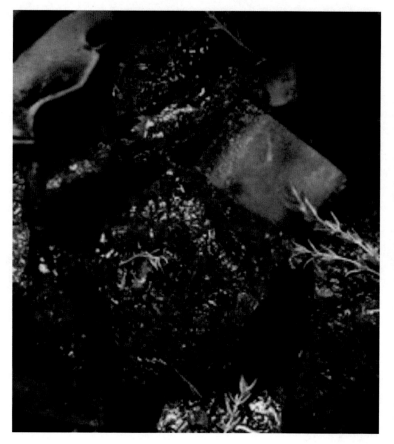

Preparation:

1. Preheat the unit by selecting AIR FRY mode for 5 minutes at 325 degrees F.
2. Select START/PAUSE to begin the preheating process.
3. Once preheating is done, press START/PAUSE.
4. Season the ribs with salt and black pepper and rub a little amount of canola oil on both sides.
5. Place it in the basket of the air fryer.
6. Next, take a bowl and add pearl onions, parsnip, carrots, garlic, brown sugar, red wine, salt, and black pepper.
7. Add the vegetable mixture over the ribs.
8. Set the basket time to 45 minutes at 390 degrees F at AIR FRY mode.
9. Hit start so the cooking cycle being.
10. Once the cooking complete, take out the ingredient and serve short ribs with the mixed vegetables and liquid collect at the bottom of basket.
11. Enjoy it hot.

Serving Suggestion: Serve it with mashed potatoes

Variation Tip: Use olive oil instead of canola oil.

Nutritional Information Per Serving:

Calories 1262| Fat 98.6g| Sodium 595mg| Carbs 57g| Fiber 10.1g| Sugar 28.2g| Protein 35.8g

Chinese BBQ Pork

Prep Time: 15 minutes.
Cook Time: 25-35 minutes.
Serves: 2

Sauce Ingredients:

- 4 tablespoons of soy sauce
- ¼ cup red wine
- 2 tablespoons of oyster sauce
- ¼ tablespoons of hoisin sauce
- ¼ cup honey
- ¼ cup brown sugar
- Pinch of salt
- Pinch of black pepper
- 1 teaspoon of ginger garlic, paste
- 1 teaspoon of five-spice powder

Other Ingredients:

- 1.5 pounds of pork shoulder, sliced

Preparation:

1. Take a bowl and mix all the ingredients listed under sauce ingredients.
2. Transfer half of it to a sauce pan and let it cook for 10 minutes.
3. Set it aside.
4. Let the pork marinate in the remaining sauce for 2 hours.
5. Afterward, put the pork slices in the basket and set it to AIRFRY mode 450 degrees for 25 minutes.

6. Make sure the internal temperature is above 160 degrees F once cooked.
7. If not add a few more minutes to the overall cooking time.
8. Once done, take it out and baste it with prepared sauce.
9. Serve and Enjoy.

Serving Suggestion: Serve it with rice

Variation Tip: Skip the wine and add vinegar

Nutritional Information Per Serving:

Calories 1239| Fat 73g| Sodium 2185mg| Carbs 57.3g| Fiber 0.4g| Sugar 53.7g| Protein 81.5g

Glazed Steak Recipe

Prep Time: 15 minutes.

Cook Time: 25 minutes.

Serves: 2

Ingredients:

- 1 pound of beef steaks
- ½ cup, soy sauce

- Salt and black pepper, to taste
- 1 tablespoon of vegetable oil
- 1 teaspoon of grated ginger
- 4 cloves garlic, minced
- 1/4 cup brown sugar

Preparation:

1. Take a bowl and whisk together soy sauce, salt, pepper, vegetable oil, garlic, brown sugar, and ginger.
2. Once a paste is made rub the steak with the marinate
3. Let it sit for 30 minutes.
4. After 30 minutes add the steak to the air fryer basket and set it to AIR FRY mode at 400 degrees F for 18-22 minutes.
5. After 10 minutes, hit pause and takeout the basket.
6. Let the steak flip and again let it AIR FRY for the remaining minutes.
7. Once 25 minutes of cooking cycle completes.
8. Take out the steak and let it rest. Serve by cutting into slices.
9. Enjoy.

Serving Suggestion: Serve it with mashed potatoes

Variation Tip: Use canola oil instead of vegetable oil

Nutritional Information Per Serving:

Calories 563| Fat 21g| Sodium 156mg| Carbs 20.6g| Fiber 0.3g| Sugar 17.8g| Protein 69.4g

Steak and Mashed Creamy Potatoes

Prep Time: 15 minutes.

Cook Time: 45-50 minutes.

Serves: 1

Ingredients:

- 2 Russet potatoes, peeled and cubed
- ¼ cup butter, divided
- 1/3 cup heavy cream
- ½ cup shredded cheddar cheese
- Salt and black pepper, to taste
- 1 New York strip steak, about a pound
- 1 teaspoon of olive oil

- Oil spray, for greasing

Preparation:
1. Preheat the unit by selecting AIR FRY mode for 5 minutes at 350 degrees F.
2. Select START/PAUSE to begin the preheating process.
3. Once preheating is done, press START/PAUSE.
4. Rub the potatoes with salt and a little amount of olive oil about a teaspoon.
5. Next, season the steak with salt and black pepper.
6. Place the russet potatoes along with steak in basket of air fryer.
7. Oil sprays the steak and set it to AIR fry mode for 50 minutes, at 375 degrees F.
8. Hit start and Lethe ninja Foodi do its magic.
9. One 12 minutes pass, take out the steak and let the cooking cycle completes.
10. Afterward take out potato and mash the potatoes and then add butter, heavy cream, and cheese along with salt and black pepper.
11. Serve the mashed potatoes with steak.
12. Enjoy.

Serving Suggestion: Serve it with rice

Variation Tip: Use Parmesan instead of cheddar

Nutritional Information Per Serving:

Calories 1932| Fat 85.2g| Sodium 3069mg| Carbs 82g| Fiber 10.3g| Sugar 5.3g| Protein 22.5g

Steak in Air Fry

Prep Time: 15 minutes.

Cook Time: 22 minutes.

Serves: 1

Ingredients:
- 2 teaspoons of canola oil
- 1 tablespoon of Montreal steaks seasoning
- 1 pound of beef steak

Preparation:
1. The first step is to season the steak on both sides with canola oil and then rub a generous amount of steak seasoning all over.

2. Put the steak in the basket and set it to AIR FRY mode at 450 degrees F for 22 minutes.
3. After 7 minutes, hit pause and take out the basket to flip the steak, and cover it with foil on top, for the remaining 14 minutes.
4. Once done, serve the medium-rare steak and enjoy it by resting for 10 minutes.
5. Serve by cutting in slices.

6. Enjoy.

Serving Suggestion: Serve it with mashed potatoes

Variation Tip: Use vegetable oil instead of canola oil.

Nutritional Information Per Serving:

Calories 935| Fat 37.2g| Sodium 1419mg| Carbs 0g| Fiber 0g| Sugar 0g| Protein 137.5g

Beef & Broccoli

Prep Time: 12 minutes.

Cook Time: 12 minutes.

Serves: 4

Ingredients:

- 12 ounces of teriyaki sauce, divided
- ½ tablespoon garlic powder
- ¼ cup of soy sauce
- 1 pound raw sirloin steak, thinly sliced
- 2 cups broccoli, cut into florets
- 2 teaspoons of olive oil
- Salt and black pepper, to taste

Preparation:

1. Preheat the unit by selecting AIR FRY mode for 7 minutes at 350 degrees F.
2. Select START/PAUSE to begin the preheating process.
3. Once preheating is done, press START/PAUSE.
4. Take a zip-lock plastic bag and mix teriyaki sauce, salt, garlic powder, black pepper, soy sauce, and olive oil.
5. Marinate the beef in it for 2 hours.
6. Then drain the beef from the marinade.
7. Now toss the broccoli with oil, teriyaki sauce, and salt and black pepper.
8. Put the ingredients inside the air fryer basket.
9. Set it to AIRFRY mode at 390 degrees F, for 12 minutes.
10. Hit start and let the cooking cycle completes.
11. Once it's done take out the beef and broccoli and serve immediately with leftover teriyaki sauce and cooked rice.

Serving Suggestion: Serve it with mashed potatoes

Variation Tip: Use canola oil instead of olive oil

Nutritional Information Per Serving:

Calories 344| Fat 10g| Sodium 4285mg| Carbs 18.2g| Fiber 1.5g| Sugar 13.3g| Protein 42g

Yogurt Lamb Chops

Prep Time: 10 minutes.

Cook Time: 22 minutes.

Serves: 2

Ingredients:

- 1½ cups plain Greek yogurt
- 1 lemon, juice only
- 1 teaspoon ground cumin
- 1 teaspoon ground coriander
- ¾teaspoon ground turmeric
- ¼ teaspoon ground allspice
- 10 rib lamb chops (1–1¼ inches thick cut)
- 2 tablespoons olive oil, divided

Preparation:

1. Take a bowl and add lamb chop along with listed ingredients.
2. Rub the lamb chops well.
3. and let it marinate in the refrigerator for 1 hour.
4. Afterward takeout the lamb chops from the refrigerator.
5. Layer parchment paper inside basket
6. Put the chops inside basket and place the basket inside the unit.
7. Set the time to 22 minutes at 400 degrees F.
8. Hit start and then wait for the chop to be cooked.
9. Once the cooking is done, take out the lamb chops and let the chops serve on plates.

Serving Suggestion: Serve over rice

Variation Tip: Use canola oil instead of olive oil

Nutritional Information Per Serving:

Calories 1973| Fat 90g| Sodium 228mg| Carbs 109.2g| Fiber 1g| Sugar 77.5g| Protein 184g

Beef Ribs I

Prep Time: 10 minutes.

Cook Time: 18 minutes.

Serves: 2

Ingredients:

- 4 tablespoons of barbecue spice rub
- 1 tablespoon kosher salt and black pepper
- 3 tablespoons brown sugar
- 2 pounds of beef ribs (3-3 1/2 pounds), cut in thirds
- 1 cup barbecue sauce

Preparation:

1. In a small bowl, add salt, pepper, brown sugar, and BBQ spice rub.
2. Grease the ribs with oil spray from both sides and then rub it with a spice mixture.

3. Adjust the ribs inside the Ninja Air fryer, and set it to AIR FRY MODE at 375 degrees F for 18 minutes.
4. Hit start and let the air fryer cook the ribs.
5. Once done, serve with the coating BBQ sauce.

Serving Suggestion: Serve it with salad and baked potato

Variation Tip: Use sea salt instead of kosher salt

Nutritional Information Per Serving:

Calories 1081| Fat 28.6g| Sodium 1701mg| Carbs 58g| Fiber 0.8g| Sugar 45.7g| Protein 138g

Beef Ribs II

Prep Time: 20 minutes.

Cook Time: 1 Hour.

Serves: 2

Ingredients for Marinade:

- ¼ cup olive oil
- 4 garlic cloves, minced
- ½ cup white wine vinegar
- ¼ cup soy sauce, reduced-sodium
- ¼ cup Worcestershire sauce
- 1 lemon juice
- Salt and black pepper, to taste
- 2 tablespoons of Italian seasoning
- 1 teaspoon of smoked paprika
- 2 tablespoons of mustard
- ½ cup maple syrup

Meat Ingredients:

- Oil spray, for greasing
- 8 beef ribs lean

Preparation:

1. Preheat the unit by selecting AIR FRY mode for 2 minutes at 325 degrees F.
2. Select START/PAUSE to begin the preheating process.
3. Once preheating is done, press START/PAUSE.
1. Take a large bowl and add all the ingredients under marinade ingredients.
2. Put the marinade in a zip lock bag and add ribs to it.
3. Let it sit for 4 hours.
4. Now take out the basket of air fryer and grease the basket with oil spray.
5. Now put the ribs in the basket.
6. Set it to AIR fry mode at 220 degrees F for 30 minutes.
7. Select Pause and take out the basket.
8. Afterward, flip the ribs and cook for 30 more minutes at 250 degrees F.
9. Once done, serve the juicy and tender ribs.
10. Enjoy.

Serving Suggestion: Serve it with Mac and cheese

Variation Tip: Use garlic-infused oil instead of garlic cloves

Nutritional Information Per Serving:

Calories 1927| Fat 116g| Sodium 1394mg| Carbs 35.2g| Fiber 1.3g| Sugar 29g| Protein 172.3g

Crumbed Chicken Katsu

Prep Time: 15 minutes.

Cook Time: 26 minutes.

Serves: 4

Ingredients:

- 1 lb boneless chicken breast, cut in half
- 2 large eggs, beaten
- 1 ½ cups panko bread crumbs
- Salt and black pepper ground to taste
- Cooking spray

Sauce:

- 1 tablespoon sugar
- 2 tablespoons soy sauce
- 1 tablespoon sherry
- ½ cup ketchup
- 2 teaspoons Worcestershire sauce
- 1 teaspoon garlic, minced

Preparation:

1. At 390 degrees F, preheat your Air Fryer on Air fry mode.
2. Mix soy sauce, ketchup, sherry, sugar, garlic, and Worcestershire sauce in a mixing bowl.
3. Keep this katsu aside for a while.
4. Rub the chicken pieces with salt and black pepper.
5. Whisk eggs in a shallow dish and spread breadcrumbs in another tray.
6. Dip the chicken in the egg mixture and coat them with breadcrumbs.
7. Place the coated chicken in the Air Fryer Basket and spray them with cooking spray.
8. Return the Air Fryer Basket to the Air Fryer and cook for 26 minutes.
9. Initiate cooking by pressing the START/PAUSE BUTTON.
10. Flip the chicken once cooked halfway through, then resume cooking.
11. Serve warm with the sauce

Serving Suggestion: Serve with fried rice and green beans salad.

Variation Tip: Coat the chicken with crushed cornflakes for extra crispiness.

Nutritional Information Per Serving:

Calories 220 | Fat 1.7g |Sodium 178mg | Carbs 1.7g | Fiber 0.2g | Sugar 0.2g | Protein 32.9g

Pickled Chicken Fillets

Prep Time: 15 minutes.

Cook Time: 28 minutes.

Serves: 4

Ingredients:

- 2 boneless chicken breasts
- 1/2 cup dill pickle juice
- 2 eggs
- 1/2 cup milk
- 1 cup flour, all-purpose
- 2 tablespoons powdered sugar
- 2 tablespoons potato starch
- 1 teaspoon paprika
- 1 teaspoon of sea salt
- 1/2 teaspoons black pepper
- 1/2 teaspoons garlic powder
- 1/4 teaspoons ground celery seed ground
- 1 tablespoon olive oil

- Cooking spray
- 4 hamburger buns, toasted
- 8 dill pickle chips

Preparation:

1. At 390 degrees F, preheat your Air Fryer on Air fry mode.
2. Set the chicken in a suitable Ziplock bag and pound it into ½ thickness with a mallet.
3. Slice the chicken into 2 halves.
4. Add pickle juice and seal the bag.
5. Refrigerate for 30 minutes approximately for marination. Whisk both eggs with milk in a shallow bowl.
6. Thoroughly mix flour with spices and flour in a separate bowl.
7. Dip each chicken slice in egg, then in the flour mixture.
8. Shake off the excess and set the chicken pieces in the Air Fryer Basket.
9. Spray the pieces with cooking oil.
10. Place the chicken pieces in the Air Fryer Basket in a single layer and spray the cooking oil.
11. Return the Air Fryer Basket to the Air Fryer and cook for 28 minutes.
12. Initiate cooking by pressing the START/PAUSE BUTTON.
13. Flip the chicken pieces once cooked halfway through, and resume cooking.
14. Enjoy with pickle chips and a dollop of mayonnaise.

Serving Suggestion: Serve with warm corn tortilla and Greek salad.

Variation Tip: You can use the almond flour breading for a low-carb serving.

Nutritional Information Per Serving:

Calories 353 | Fat 5g |Sodium 818mg | Carbs 53.2g | Fiber 4.4g | Sugar 8g | Protein 17.3g

Crusted Chicken Breast

Prep Time: 15 minutes.

Cook Time: 28 minutes.

Serves: 4

Ingredients:

- 2 large eggs, beaten
- 1/2 cup all-purpose flour
- 1 1/4 cup panko bread crumbs
- 2/3 cup Parmesan, grated
- 4 teaspoons lemon zest
- 2 teaspoons dried oregano
- Salt, to taste
- 1 teaspoon cayenne pepper
- Freshly black pepper, to taste
- 4 boneless skinless chicken breasts

Preparation:

1. At 390 degrees F, preheat your Air Fryer on Air fry mode.
2. Beat eggs in one shallow bowl and spread flour in another shallow bowl.
3. Mix panko with oregano, lemon zest, Parmesan, cayenne, oregano, salt, and black pepper in another shallow bowl.
4. First, coat the chicken with flour first, then dip it in the eggs and coat them with panko mixture.
5. Arrange the prepared chicken in the Air Fryer Basket.
6. Return the Air Fryer Basket to the Air Fryer and cook for 28 minutes.
7. Initiate cooking by pressing the START/PAUSE BUTTON.
8. Flip the half-cooked chicken and continue cooking until golden.
9. Serve warm

Serving Suggestion: Serve with fresh-cut tomatoes and sautéed greens.

Variation Tip: Rub the chicken with lemon juice before seasoning.

Nutritional Information Per Serving:

Calories 220 | Fat 13g |Sodium 542mg | Carbs 0.9g | Fiber 0.3g | Sugar 0.2g | Protein 25.6g

Chili Chicken Wings

Prep Time: 20 minutes.

Cook Time: 43 minutes.

Serves: 4

Ingredients:

- 8 chicken wings drumettes
- cooking spray
- 1/8 cup low-fat buttermilk
- 1/4 cup almond flour
- McCormick Chicken Seasoning to taste

Thai Chili Marinade:

- 1 1/2 tablespoons low-sodium soy sauce
- ½ teaspoon ginger, minced
- 1 1/2 garlic cloves
- 1 green onion
- ½ teaspoon of rice wine vinegar
- ½ tablespoons Sriracha sauce
- ½ tablespoons sesame oil

Preparation:

1. At 390 degrees F, preheat your Air Fryer on Air fry mode.
2. Put all the ingredients for the marinade in the blender and blend them for 1 minute.
3. Keep this marinade aside. Pat dry the washed chicken and place it in the Ziploc bag.
4. Add buttermilk, chicken seasoning, and zip the bag.
5. Shake the bag well, then refrigerator for 30 minutes for marination.
6. Remove the chicken drumettes from the marinade, then dredge them through dry flour.
7. Spread the drumettes in the Air Fryer Basket and spray them with cooking oil.
8. Return the Air Fryer Basket to the Air Fryer and cook for 43 minutes.
9. Initiate cooking by pressing the START/PAUSE BUTTON.
10. Toss the drumettes once cooked halfway through.
11. Now brush the chicken pieces with Thai chili sauce and then resume cooking
12. Serve warm

Serving Suggestion: Serve with warm corn tortilla and ketchup.

Variation Tip: Rub the wings with lemon or orange juice before cooking.

Nutritional Information Per Serving:

Calories 223| Fat 11.7g | Sodium 721mg |Carbs 13.6g |Fiber 0.7g |Sugar 8g |Protein 15.7g

Chicken Potatoes

Prep Time: 10 minutes.

Cook Time: 22 minutes.

Serves: 4

Ingredients:

- 15 ounces canned potatoes drained
- 1 teaspoon olive oil
- 1 teaspoon Lawry's seasoned salt
- 1/8 teaspoons black pepper optional
- 8 ounces boneless chicken breast cubed
- 1/4 teaspoons paprika
- 3/8 cup cheddar, shredded
- 4 bacon slices, cooked, cut into strips

Preparation:

1. At 300 degrees F, preheat your Air Fryer on Air fry mode.
2. Dice the chicken into small pieces and toss them with olive oil and spices.
3. Drain and dice the potato pieces into smaller cubes.
4. Add potato to the chicken and mix well to coat.
5. Spread the mixture in the Air Fryer Basket in a single layer.
6. Return the Air Fryer Basket to the Air Fryer and cook for 22 minutes.
7. Top the chicken and potatoes with cheese and bacon.
8. Return the Air Fryer Basket to the Air Fryer.
9. Select the Air Broil mode with 300 degrees F temperature and 5 minutes cooking time.
10. Initiate cooking by pressing the START/PAUSE BUTTON.
11. Enjoy with dried herbs on top.

Serving Suggestion: Serve with boiled white rice.

Variation Tip: Add sweet potatoes and green beans instead of potatoes.

Nutritional Information Per Serving:

Calories 346| Fat 16.1g|Sodium 882mg| Carbs 1.3g| Fiber 0.5g| Sugar 0.5g| Protein 48.2g

Air Fried Turkey Breast

Prep Time: 10 minutes.

Cook Time: 46 minutes.

Serves: 4

Ingredients:

- 2 lbs. turkey breast, on the bone with skin
- ½ tablespoons olive oil

- 1 teaspoon salt
- 1/4 tablespoons dry poultry seasoning

Preparation:

1. At 390 degrees F, preheat your Air Fryer on Air fry mode.
2. Rub turkey breast with ½ tablespoons oil.
3. Season both its sides with turkey seasoning and salt, then rub in the brush half tablespoons of oil over the skin of the turkey.
4. Place the turkey in the Air Fryer Basket.
5. Return the Air Fryer Basket to the Air Fryer and cook for 46 minutes.
6. Initiate cooking by pressing the START/PAUSE BUTTON.
7. Flip the turkey once cooked halfway through, and resume cooking.
8. Slice and serve warm.

Serving Suggestion: Serve with warm corn tortilla and Greek salad.

Variation Tip: Coat and dust the turkey breast with flour after seasoning.

Nutritional Information Per Serving:

Calories 502 | Fat 25g |Sodium 230mg | Carbs 1.5g | Fiber 0.2g | Sugar 0.4g | Protein 64.1g

Chicken Drumettes

Prep Time: 15 minutes.

Cook Time: 52 minutes.

Serves: 5

Ingredients:

- 10 large chicken drumettes
- Cooking spray
- ¼ cup of rice vinegar
- 3 tablespoons honey
- 2 tablespoons unsalted chicken stock
- 1 tablespoon soy sauce
- 1 tablespoon toasted sesame oil
- 3/8 teaspoons crushed red pepper

- 1 garlic clove, chopped
- 2 tablespoons chopped unsalted roasted peanuts
- 1 tablespoon chopped fresh chives

Preparation:

1. At 390 degrees F, preheat your Air Fryer on Air fry mode.
2. Spread the chicken in the Air Fryer Basket in an even layer and spray cooking spray on top.
3. Return the Air Fryer Basket to the Air Fryer and cook for 47 minutes.
4. Initiate cooking by pressing the START/PAUSE BUTTON.
5. Flip the chicken drumettes once cooked halfway through, then resume cooking.
6. During this time, mix soy sauce, honey, stock, vinegar, garlic, and crushed red pepper in a suitable saucepan and place it over medium-high heat to cook on a simmer.
7. Cook this sauce for 6 minutes with occasional stirring, then pour it into a medium-sized bowl.
8. Add Air fried drumettes and toss well to coat with the honey sauce.
9. Garnish with chives and peanuts.
10. Serve warm and fresh

Serving Suggestion: Serve with tomato ketchup or chili sauce.

Variation Tip: Rub the chicken with lemon juice before seasoning.

Nutritional Information Per Serving:

Calories 268| Fat 10.4g| Sodium 411mg| Carbs 0.4g| Fiber 0.1g| Sugar 0.1g| Protein 40.6g

Brazilian Chicken Drumsticks

Prep Time: 15 minutes.

Cook Time: 27 minutes.

Serves: 6

Ingredients:

- 2 teaspoons cumin seeds
- 2 teaspoons dried parsley
- 2 teaspoons turmeric powder
- 2 teaspoons dried oregano leaves
- 2 teaspoons salt
- 1 teaspoon coriander seeds
- 1 teaspoon black peppercorns
- 1 teaspoon cayenne pepper
- 1/2 cup lime juice
- 4 tablespoons vegetable oil
- 3 lbs chicken drumsticks

Preparation:

1. At 390 degrees F, preheat your Air Fryer on Air fry mode.
2. Grind cumin, parsley, salt, coriander seeds, cayenne pepper, peppercorns, oregano, and turmeric in a food processor.

3. Add this mixture to lemon juice and oil in a bowl and mix well.
4. Rub the spice paste over the chicken drumsticks and let them marinate for 30 minutes.
5. Place the chicken drumsticks in the Air Fryer Basket.
6. Return the Air Fryer Basket to the Air Fryer and cook for 27 minutes.
7. Initiate cooking by pressing the START/PAUSE BUTTON.
8. Flip the drumsticks when cooked halfway through, then resume cooking.
9. Serve warm.

Serving Suggestion: Serve with tomato ketchup or chili sauce.

Variation Tip: Use buttermilk to soak the drumsticks before seasoning.

Nutritional Information Per Serving:

Calories 456| Fat 16.4g| Sodium 1321mg| Carbs 19.2g| Fiber 2.2g| Sugar 4.2g| Protein 55.2g

Bang-Bang Chicken

Prep Time: 15 minutes.

Cook Time: 20 minutes.

Serves: 2

Ingredients:

* 1 cup mayonnaise
* ½ cup sweet chili sauce
* 2 tablespoons Sriracha sauce
* ⅓ cup flour
* 1 lb boneless chicken breast, diced
* 1 ½ cups panko bread crumbs
* 2 green onions, chopped

Preparation:

1. At 390 degrees F, preheat your Air Fryer on Air fry mode.

2. Mix mayonnaise with Sriracha and sweet chili sauce in a large bowl.

3. Keep 3/4 cup of the mixture aside.

4. Add flour, chicken, breadcrumbs, and remaining mayo mixture to a resealable plastic bag.

5. Zip the bag and shake well to coat.

6. Place the chicken in the Air Fryer Basket in a single layer.
7. Return the Air Fryer Basket to the Air Fryer and cook for 20 minutes.
8. Initiate cooking by pressing the START/PAUSE BUTTON.
9. Flip the chicken once cooked halfway through.
10. Top the chicken with reserved mayo sauce.
11. Garnish with green onions and serve warm

Serving Suggestion: Serve with tomato ketchup or chili sauce.

Variation Tip: Use crushed cornflakes for breading to have extra crispiness.

Nutritional Information Per Serving:

Calories 374 | Fat 13g | Sodium 552mg | Carbs 25g | Fiber 1.2g | Sugar 1.2g | Protein 37.7g

Veggie Stuffed Chicken Breasts

Prep Time: 15 minutes.

Cook Time: 10 minutes.

Serves: 2

Ingredients:

- 4 teaspoons chili powder
- 4 teaspoons ground cumin
- 1 skinless, boneless chicken breast
- 2 teaspoons chipotle flakes
- 2 teaspoons Mexican oregano
- Salt and black pepper, to taste
- ½ red bell pepper, julienned
- ½ onion, julienned
- 1 fresh jalapeno pepper, julienned
- 2 teaspoons corn oil
- ½ lime, juiced

Preparation:

1. At 360 degrees F, preheat your Air Fryer on Air fry mode.
2. Slice the chicken breast in half horizontally.
3. Pound each chicken breast with a mallet into ¼ inch thickness.
4. Rub the pounded chicken breast with black pepper, salt, oregano, chipotle flakes, cumin, and chili powder.
5. Add ½ of bell pepper, jalapeno, and onion on top of each chicken breast piece.
6. Roll the chicken to wrap the filling inside and insert toothpicks to seal.
7. Place the rolls in the Air Fryer Basket and spray them with cooking oil.
8. Return the Air Fryer Basket to the Air Fryer and cook for 10 minutes.
9. Initiate cooking by pressing the START/PAUSE BUTTON.
10. Serve warm.

Serving Suggestion: Serve with tomato ketchup or chili sauce.

Variation Tip: season the chicken rolls with seasoned parmesan before cooking.

Nutritional Information Per Serving:

Calories 351 | Fat 11g | Sodium 150mg | Carbs 3.3g | Fiber 0.2g | Sugar 1g | Protein 33.2g

General Tso's Chicken

Prep Time: 20 minutes.

Cook Time: 22 minutes.

Serves: 4

Ingredients:

- 1 egg, large
- 1/3 cup 2 teaspoons cornstarch,
- 1/4 teaspoons salt
- 1/4 teaspoons ground white pepper
- 7 tablespoons chicken broth
- 2 tablespoons soy sauce
- 2 tablespoons ketchup
- 2 teaspoons sugar
- 2 teaspoons unseasoned rice vinegar
- 1 1/2 tablespoons canola oil
- 4 chilies de árbol, chopped and seeds discarded
- 1 tablespoon chopped fresh ginger
- 1 tablespoon garlic, chopped
- 2 tablespoons green onion, sliced
- 1 teaspoon toasted sesame oil
- 1 lb boneless chicken thighs, cut into 1 ¼ -inch chunks
- 1/2 teaspoons toasted sesame seeds

Preparation:

1. At 390 degrees F, preheat your Air Fryer on Air fry mode.
2. Add egg to a large bowl and beat it with a fork.
3. Add chicken to the egg and coat it well.
4. Whisk 1/3 cup cornstarch with black pepper and salt in a small bowl.
5. Add chicken to the cornstarch mixture and mix well to coat.
6. Place the chicken in the Air Fryer Basket and spray them with cooking oil.
7. Return the Air Fryer Basket to the Air Fryer and cook for 20 minutes.
8. Initiate cooking by pressing the START/PAUSE BUTTON.
9. Once done, remove the air fried chicken from the Air fryer.
10. Whisk 2 teaspoons cornstarch with soy sauce, broth, sugar, ketchup, and rice vinegar in a small bowl.
11. Add chilies and canola oil to a skillet and sauté for 1 minute.
12. Add garlic and ginger, then sauté for 30 seconds.
13. Stir in cornstarch sauce and cook until it bubbles and thickens.
14. Toss in cooked chicken and garnish with sesame oil, sesame seeds, and green onion.
15. Enjoy.

Serving Suggestion: Serve with boiled white rice or chow Mein.

Variation Tip: You can use honey instead of sugar to sweeten the sauce.

Nutritional Information Per Serving:

Calories 351 | Fat 16g | Sodium 777mg | Carbs 26g | Fiber 4g | Sugar 5g | Protein 28g

Bacon-Wrapped Chicken

Prep Time: 10 minutes.

Cook Time: 28 minutes.

Serves: 2

Ingredients:

- Butter:
- ½ stick butter softened
- ½ garlic clove, minced
- ¼ teaspoons dried thyme
- ¼ teaspoons dried basil
- ⅛ teaspoons coarse salt
- 1 pinch black pepper, ground
- ⅓ lb thick-cut bacon
- 1 ½ lbs boneless skinless chicken thighs
- 2 teaspoons garlic, minced

Preparation:

1. At 390 degrees F, preheat your Air Fryer on Air fry mode.
2. Mix garlic softened butter with thyme, salt, basil, and black pepper in a bowl.
3. Add butter mixture on a piece of wax paper and roll it up tightly to make a butter log.
4. Place the log in the refrigerator for 2 hours.
5. Spray one bacon strip on a piece of wax paper.
6. Place each chicken thigh on top of one bacon strip and rub it with garlic.
7. Make a slit in the chicken thigh and add a teaspoon of butter to the chicken.
8. Wrap the bacon around the chicken thigh.
9. Repeat those same steps with all the chicken thighs.
10. Place the bacon-wrapped chicken thighs in the Air Fryer Basket.
11. Return the Air Fryer Basket to the Air Fryer and cook for 28 minutes.
12. Initiate cooking by pressing the START/PAUSE BUTTON.
13. Flip the chicken once cooked halfway through, and resume cooking.
14. Serve warm

Serving Suggestion: Serve with tomato ketchup or chili sauce.

Variation Tip: Drizzle mixed dried herbs on top before cooking.

Nutritional Information Per Serving:

Calories 380 | Fat 29g | Sodium 821mg | Carbs 34.6g | Fiber 0g | Sugar 0g | Protein 30g

Cheddar- Stuffed Chicken

Prep Time: 10 minutes.

Cook Time: 20 minutes.

Serves: 4

Ingredients:

- 3 bacon strips, cooked and crumbled
- 2 ounces Cheddar cheese, cubed
- ¼ cup barbeque sauce
- 2 (4 ounces) boneless chicken breasts
- Salt and black pepper to taste

Preparation:

1. At 360 degrees F, preheat your Air Fryer on Air fry mode.
2. Make a 1-inch deep pouch in each chicken breast.
3. Mix cheddar cubes with half of the BBQ sauce, salt, black pepper, and bacon.
4. Divide this filling in the chicken breasts and secure the edges with a toothpick.
5. Brush the remaining BBQ sauce over the chicken breasts.
6. Place the chicken in the Air Fryer Basket and spray them with cooking oil.
7. Return the Air Fryer Basket to the Air Fryer and cook for 20 minutes.
8. Initiate cooking by pressing the START/PAUSE BUTTON.
9. Serve warm.

Serving Suggestion: Serve with tomato salsa on top.

Variation Tip: Use poultry seasoning for breading.

Nutritional Information Per Serving:

Calories 379 | Fat 19g | Sodium 184mg | Carbs 12.3g | Fiber 0.6g | Sugar 2g | Protein 37.7g

Balsamic Duck Breast

Prep Time: 15 minutes.

Cook Time: 20 minutes.

Serves: 2

Ingredients:

- 2 Duck Breasts
- 1 teaspoon parsley
- Salt and black pepper, to taste

Marinade:

- 1 tablespoon olive oil
- ½ teaspoon French mustard
- 1 teaspoon dried garlic
- 2 teaspoons honey
- ½ teaspoon Balsamic vinegar

Preparation:

1. At 360 degrees F, preheat your Air Fryer on Air fry mode.
2. Mix olive oil, mustard, garlic, honey, and balsamic vinegar in a bowl.
3. Add duck breasts to the marinade and rub well.
4. Place one duck breast in the Air Fryer Basket.
5. Return the Air Fryer Basket to the Air Fryer and cook for 20 minutes.
6. Initiate cooking by pressing the START/PAUSE BUTTON.
7. Flip the duck breasts once cooked halfway through, then resume cooking.
8. Serve warm.

Serving Suggestion: Serve with white rice and avocado salad

Variation Tip: Rub the duck breast with garlic cloves before seasoning.

Nutritional Information Per Serving:

Calories 546| Fat 33.1g| Sodium 1201mg | Carbs 30g | Fiber 2.4g | Sugar 9.7g | Protein 32g

Fish and Seafood Recipes

Salmon Nuggets

Prep Time: 15 minutes.

Cook Time: 15 minutes.

Serves: 4

Ingredients:

- ⅓ cup maple syrup
- ¼ teaspoon dried chipotle pepper
- 1 pinch sea salt
- 1 ½ cups croutons
- 1 large egg
- 1 (1 pound) skinless salmon fillet, cut into 1 1/2-inch chunk
- cooking spray

Preparation:

1. At 390 degrees F, preheat your Air Fryer on Air fry mode.
2. Mix chipotle powder, maple syrup, and salt in a saucepan and cook on a simmer for 5 minutes.
3. Crush the croutons in a food processor and transfer them to a bowl.
4. Beat egg in another shallow bowl.
5. Season the salmon chunks with sea salt.
6. Dip the salmon in the egg, then coat with breadcrumbs.
7. Spread the coated salmon chunks in the Air Fryer Basket.
8. Return the Air Fryer Basket to the Air Fryer and cook for 10 minutes.
9. Initiate cooking by pressing the START/PAUSE BUTTON.
10. Flip the chunks once cooked halfway through, then resume cooking.
11. Pour the maple syrup on top and serve warm.

Serving Suggestion: Serve with creamy dip and crispy fries.

Variation Tip: Use crushed cornflakes for breading to have extra crispiness.

Nutritional Information Per Serving:

Calories 275| Fat 1.4g| Sodium 582mg| Carbs 31.5g | Fiber 1.1g | Sugar 0.1g | Protein 29.8g

Fish Sandwich

Prep Time: 15 minutes.

Cook Time: 22 minutes.

Serves: 4

Ingredients:

- 4 small cod fillets, skinless
- Salt and black pepper, to taste

- 2 tablespoons flour
- ¼ cup dried breadcrumbs
- Spray oil
- 9 ounces of frozen peas
- 1 tablespoon creme fraiche
- 12 capers
- 1 squeeze of lemon juice
- 4 bread rolls, cut in halve

Preparation:

1. At 390 degrees F, preheat your Air Fryer on Air fry mode.
2. First, coat the cod fillets with flour, salt, and black pepper.
3. Then coat the fish with breadcrumbs.
4. Place the coated codfish in the Air Fryer Basket and spray them with cooking spray.
5. Return the Air Fryer Basket to the Air Fryer and cook for 17 minutes.
6. Initiate cooking by pressing the START/PAUSE BUTTON.
7. Meanwhile, boil peas in hot water for 5 minutes until soft.
8. Then drain the peas and transfer them to the blender.
9. Add capers, lemon juice, and crème fraiche to the blender.
10. Blend until it makes a smooth mixture.
11. Spread the peas crème mixture on top of 2 lower halves of the bread roll, and place the fish fillets on it.
12. Place the remaining bread slices on top.
13. Serve fresh

Serving Suggestion: Serve with sautéed or fresh greens with melted butter.

Variation Tip: Coat the fish with crushed cornflakes for extra crispiness.

Nutritional Information Per Serving:

Calories 348 | Fat 30g | Sodium 660mg | Carbs 5g | Fiber 0g | Sugar 0g | Protein 14g

Breaded Scallops

Prep Time: 15 minutes.

Cook Time: 12 minutes.

Serves: 4

Ingredients:

- ½ cup crushed buttery crackers
- ½ teaspoon garlic powder
- ½ teaspoon seafood seasoning
- 2 tablespoons butter, melted
- 1-pound sea scallops patted dry

- cooking spray

Preparation:

1. At 390 degrees F, preheat your Air Fryer on Air fry mode.

2. Mix cracker crumbs, garlic powder, and seafood seasoning in a shallow bowl. Spread melted butter in another shallow bowl.

3. Dip each scallop in the melted butter and then roll in the breading to coat well.

4. Grease the Air Fryer Basket with cooking spray and place the scallops inside.

5. Return the Air Fryer Basket to the Air Fryer and cook for 12 minutes.

6. Initiate cooking by pressing the START/PAUSE BUTTON.

7. Flip the scallops with a spatula after 4 minutes and resume cooking.

8. Serve warm.

Serving Suggestion: Serve with creamy dip and crispy fries.

Variation Tip: Use crushed cornflakes for breading to have extra crispiness.

Nutritional Information Per Serving:

Calories 275| Fat 1.4g| Sodium 582mg| Carbs 31.5g | Fiber 1.1g | Sugar 0.1g | Protein 29.8g

Fried Lobster Tails

Prep Time: 10 minutes.

Cook Time: 18 minutes.

Serves: 4

Ingredients:

- 4 (4 oz) lobster tails
- 8 tablespoons butter, melted
- 2 teaspoons lemon zest
- 2 garlic cloves, grated
- Salt and black pepper ground to taste
- 2 teaspoons fresh parsley, chopped
- 4 wedges lemon

Preparation:

1. At 350 degrees F, preheat your Air Fryer on Air fry mode.

2. Spread the lobster tails into Butterfly, slit the top to expose the lobster meat while keeping the tail intact.

3. Place the lobster tails in the Air Fryer Basket with their lobster meat facing up.

4. Mix melted butter with lemon zest and garlic in a bowl.

5. Brush the butter mixture on top of the lobster tails.

6. And drizzle salt and black pepper on top.

7. Return the Air Fryer Basket to the Air Fryer and cook for 18 minutes.

8. Initiate cooking by pressing the START/PAUSE BUTTON.

9. Garnish with parsley and lemon wedges.

10. Serve warm

Serving Suggestion: Serve on a bed of lettuce leaves.

Variation Tip: Drizzle crushed cornflakes on top to have extra crispiness.

Nutritional Information Per Serving:

Calories 257 | Fat 10.4g | Sodium 431mg | Carbs 20g | Fiber 0g | Sugar 1.6g | Protein 21g

Salmon Patties

Prep Time: 15 minutes.

Cook Time: 18 minutes.

Serves: 8

Ingredients:

- 1 lb fresh Atlantic salmon side
- 1/4 cup avocado, mashed
- 1/4 cup cilantro, diced
- 1 1/2 teaspoons yellow curry powder
- 1/2 teaspoons sea salt
- 1/4 cup, 4 teaspoons tapioca starch
- 2 brown eggs
- 1/2 cup coconut flakes
- Coconut oil, melted, for brushing
- For the greens:
- 2 teaspoons organic coconut oil, melted
- 6 cups arugula & spinach mix, tightly packed
- Pinch of sea salt

Preparation:

1. At 390 degrees F, preheat your Air Fryer on Air fry mode.
2. Remove the fish skin and dice the flesh.
3. Place in a large bowl. Add cilantro, avocado, salt, and curry powder mix gently.
4. Add tapioca starch and mix well again.
5. Make 8 salmon patties out of this mixture, about a half-inch thick.
6. Place them on a baking sheet lined with wax paper and freeze them for 20 minutes.
7. Place ¼ cup tapioca starch and coconut flakes on a flat plate.
8. Dip the patties in the whisked egg, then coat the frozen patties in the starch and flakes.
9. Place the patties in the Air Fryer Basket and spray them with cooking oil
10. Return the Air Fryer Basket to the Air Fryer and cook for 17 minutes.
11. Initiate cooking by pressing the START/PAUSE BUTTON.
12. Flip the patties once cooked halfway through, then resume cooking.
13. Sauté arugula with spinach in coconut oil in a pan for 30 seconds.
14. Serve the patties with sautéed greens mixture

Serving Suggestion: Serve with sautéed green beans or asparagus.

Variation Tip: Add lemon juice to the mixture before mixing.

Nutritional Information Per Serving:

Calories 260 | Fat 16g | Sodium 585mg | Carbs 3.1g | Fiber 1.3g | Sugar 0.2g | Protein 25.5g

Glazed Scallops

Prep Time: 15 minutes.

Cook Time: 13 minutes.

Serves: 6

Ingredients:

- 12 scallops
- 3 tablespoons olive oil
- Black pepper and salt to taste

Preparation:

1. At 390 degrees F, preheat your Air Fryer on Air fry mode.
2. Rub the scallops with olive oil, black pepper, and salt.
3. Place the scallops in the Air Fryer Basket.
4. Return the Air Fryer Basket to the Air Fryer and cook for 13 minutes.
5. Initiate cooking by pressing the START/PAUSE BUTTON.
6. Flip the scallops once cooked halfway through, and resume cooking.
7. Serve warm

Serving Suggestion: Serve with melted butter on top.

Variation Tip: Drizzle breadcrumbs on top before Air Frying.

Nutritional Information Per Serving:

Calories 308 | Fat 24g | Sodium 715mg | Carbs 0.8g | Fiber 0.1g | Sugar 0.1g | Protein 21.9g

Salmon with Fennel Salad

Prep Time: 10 minutes.

Cook Time: 17 minutes.

Serves: 4

Ingredients:

- 2 teaspoons fresh parsley, chopped
- 1 teaspoon fresh thyme, chopped
- 1 teaspoon salt
- 4 (6-oz) skinless center-cut salmon fillets
- 2 tablespoons olive oil
- 4 cups fennel, sliced
- 2/3 cup Greek yogurt
- 1 garlic clove, grated

- 2 tablespoons orange juice
- 1 teaspoon lemon juice
- 2 tablespoons fresh dill, chopped

Preparation:

1. At 390 degrees F, preheat your Air Fryer on Air fry mode.
2. Mix ½ teaspoon salt, thyme, and parsley in a small bowl.
3. Brush the salmon with oil first, then rub liberally rub the herb mixture.
4. Place salmon fillets in the Air Fryer Basket.
5. Return the Air Fryer Basket to the Air Fryer and cook for 17 minutes.
6. Initiate cooking by pressing the START/PAUSE BUTTON.
7. Meanwhile, mix fennel with garlic, yogurt, lemon juice, orange juice, remaining salt, and dill in a mixing bowl.
8. Serve the Air Fried Salmon fillets with fennel salad.
9. Enjoy.

Serving Suggestion: Serve with melted butter on top.

Variation Tip: Rub the salmon with lemon juice before cooking.

Nutritional Information Per Serving:

Calories 305 | Fat 15g | Sodium 482mg | Carbs 17g | Fiber 3g | Sugar 2g | Protein 35g

Crusted Tilapia

Prep Time: 20 minutes.

Cook Time: 17 minutes.

Serves: 4

Ingredients:

- 3/4 cup breadcrumbs
- 1 packet dry ranch-style dressing
- 2 1/2 tablespoons vegetable oil
- 2 eggs beaten
- 4 tilapia fillets
- Herbs and chilies to garnish

Preparation:

1. At 390 degrees F, preheat your Air Fryer on Air fry mode.
2. Thoroughly mix ranch dressing with panko in a bowl.
3. Whisk eggs in a shallow bowl.
4. Dip each fish fillet in the egg, then coat evenly with the panko mixture.
5. Set two coated fillets in the Air Fryer Basket.

6. Return the Air Fryer Basket to the Air Fryer and cook for 17 minutes.

7. Initiate cooking by pressing the START/PAUSE BUTTON.

8. Serve warm with herbs and chilies

Serving Suggestion: Serve with sautéed asparagus on the side.

Variation Tip: Coat the fish with crushed cornflakes for extra crispiness.

Nutritional Information Per Serving:

Calories 196| Fat 7.1g| Sodium 492mg| Carbs 21.6g| Fiber 2.9g| Sugar 0.8g| Protein 13.4g

Scallops with Greens

Prep Time: 15 minutes.

Cook Time: 13 minutes.

Serves: 8

Ingredients:

- 3/4 cup heavy whipping cream
- 1 tablespoon tomato paste
- 1 tablespoon chopped fresh basil
- 1 teaspoon garlic, minced
- 1/2 teaspoons salt
- 1/2 teaspoons pepper
- 12 ounces frozen spinach thawed
- 8 jumbo sea scallops
- Vegetable oil to spray

Preparation:

1. At 390 degrees F, preheat your Air Fryer on Air fry mode.

2. Season the scallops with vegetable oil, salt, and pepper in a bowl

3. Mix cream with spinach, basil, garlic, salt, pepper, and tomato paste in a bowl.

4. Pour this mixture over the scallops and mix gently.

5. Place the scallops in the Air Fryers Basket without using the crisper plate.

6. Return the Air Fryer Basket to the Air Fryer and cook for 13 minutes.

7. Initiate cooking by pressing the START/PAUSE BUTTON.

8. Serve right away

Serving Suggestion: Serve with fresh cucumber salad.

Variation Tip: Use crushed cornflakes for breading to have extra crispiness.

Nutritional Information Per Serving:

Calories 266| Fat 6.3g| Sodium 193mg| Carbs 39.1g | Fiber 7.2g | Sugar 5.2g | Protein 14.8g

Crusted Cod

Prep Time: 15 minutes.

Cook Time: 13 minutes.

Serves: 4

Ingredients:

- 2 lbs cod fillets
- Salt, to taste
- Freshly black pepper, to taste
- ½ cup all-purpose flour
- 1 large egg, beaten
- 2 cups panko bread crumbs
- 1 teaspoon Old Bay seasoning
- Lemon wedges, for serving
- Tartar sauce, for serving

Preparation:

1. At 390 degrees F, preheat your Air Fryer on Air fry mode.
2. Rub the fish with salt and black pepper.
3. Add flour in one shallow bowl, beat eggs in another bowl, and mix panko with Old Bay in a shallow bowl.
4. First, coat the fish with flour, then dip it in the eggs and finally coat it with the panko mixture.
5. Place the seasoned codfish in the Air Fryer Basket.
6. Return the Air Fryer Basket to the Air Fryer and cook for 13 minutes.
7. Initiate cooking by pressing the START/PAUSE BUTTON.
8. Flip the fish once cooked halfway, then resume cooking.
9. Serve warm and fresh with tartar sauce and lemon wedges.

Serving Suggestion: Enjoy with creamy coleslaw on the side.

Variation Tip: Use crushed cornflakes for extra crispiness.

Nutritional Information Per Serving:

Calories 155| Fat 4.2g | Sodium 963mg | Carbs 21.5g | Fiber 0.8g | Sugar 5.7g | Protein 8.1g

Buttered Mahi Mahi

Prep Time: 15 minutes.

Cook Time: 22 minutes.

Serves: 4

Ingredients:

- 4 (6 oz) mahi-mahi fillets
- Salt and black pepper ground to taste

- Cooking spray
- ⅔ cup butter

Preparation:

1. At 390 degrees F, preheat your Air Fryer on Air fry mode.
2. Rub the Mahi-mahi fillets with salt and black pepper.
3. Place mahi-mahi fillets in the Air Fryer's Basket.
4. Return the Air Fryer Basket to the Air Fryer and cook for 17 minutes.
5. Initiate cooking by pressing the START/PAUSE BUTTON.
6. Add butter to a saucepan and cook for 5 minutes until slightly brown.
7. Remove the butter from the heat.
8. Drizzle butter over the fish and serve warm.

Serving Suggestion: Serve with pasta or fried rice.

Variation Tip: Drizzle parmesan cheese on top.

Nutritional Information Per Serving:

Calories 399 | Fat 16g | Sodium 537mg | Carbs 28g | Fiber 3g | Sugar 10g | Protein 35g

Crusted Shrimp

Prep Time: 20 minutes.

Cook Time: 13 minutes.

Serves: 4

Ingredients:

- 1 lb shrimp
- 1/2 cup flour, all-purpose
- 1 teaspoon salt
- 1/2 teaspoons baking powder
- 2/3 cup water
- 2 cups coconut shred
- 1/2 cup bread crumbs

Preparation:

1. At 390 degrees F, preheat your Air Fryer on Air fry mode.
2. In a small bowl, whisk together flour, salt, water, and baking powder. Set aside for 5 minutes.
3. In another shallow bowl, toss bread crumbs with coconut shreds together.
4. Dredge shrimp in liquid, then coat in coconut mixture, making sure it's totally covered.
5. Repeat until all shrimp are coated.

6. Spread the shrimp in the Air Fryer Basket and spray them with cooking oil.
7. Return the Air Fryer Basket to the Air Fryer and cook for 13 minutes.
8. Initiate cooking by pressing the START/PAUSE BUTTON.
9. Shake the basket once cooked halfway, then resume cooking.
10. Serve with your favorite dip.

Serving Suggestion: Serve on top of mashed potato or mashed cauliflower.

Variation Tip: Use crushed cornflakes for breading to have extra crispiness.

Nutritional Information Per Serving:

Calories 297 | Fat 1g | Sodium 291mg | Carbs 35g | Fiber 1g | Sugar 9g | Protein 29g

Crispy Catfish

Prep Time: 15 minutes.

Cook Time: 17 minutes.

Serves: 4

Ingredients:

- 4 catfish fillets
- 1/4 cup Louisiana Fish fry
- 1 tablespoon olive oil
- 1 tablespoon parsley, chopped
- 1 lemon, sliced
- Fresh herbs to garnish

Preparation:

1. At 390 degrees F, preheat your Air Fryer on Air fry mode.
2. Mix fish fry with olive oil, and parsley then liberally rub over the catfish.

3. Place two fillets in the Air Fryer Basket.
4. Return the Air Fryer Basket to the Air Fryer and cook for 17 minutes.
5. Initiate cooking by pressing the START/PAUSE BUTTON.
6. Garnish with lemon slices and herbs.
7. Serve warm

Serving Suggestion: Serve with creamy dip and crispy fries.

Variation Tip: Use crushed cornflakes for breading to have extra crispiness.

Nutritional Information Per Serving:

Calories 275| Fat 1.4g| Sodium 582mg | Carbs 31.5g | Fiber 1.1g| Sugar 0.1g| Protein 29.8g

Savory Salmon Fillets

Prep Time: 10 minutes.

Cook Time: 17 minutes.

Serves: 4

Ingredients:

- 4 (6-oz) salmon fillets
- Salt, to taste
- Black pepper, to taste
- 4 teaspoons olive oil
- 4 tablespoons wholegrain mustard
- 2 tablespoons packed brown sugar
- 2 garlic cloves, minced
- 1 teaspoon thyme leaves

Preparation:

1. At 390 degrees F, preheat your Air Fryer on Air fry mode.
2. Rub the salmon with salt and black pepper first.
3. Whisk oil with sugar, thyme, garlic, and mustard in a small bowl.
4. Place salmon fillets in the Air Fryer Basket and brush the thyme mixture on top of each fillet.
5. Return the Air Fryer Basket to the Air Fryer and cook for 17 minutes.
6. Initiate cooking by pressing the START/PAUSE BUTTON.
7. Serve warm and fresh

Serving Suggestion: Serve with parsley and melted butter on top.

Variation Tip: Rub the fish fillets with lemon juice before cooking.

Nutritional Information Per Serving:

Calories 336 | Fat 6g | Sodium 181mg | Carbs 1.3g | Fiber 0.2g | Sugar 0.4g | Protein 69.2g

Desserts Recipes

Cake in The Air Fryer

Prep Time: 12 minutes.

Cook Time: 30 minutes.

Serves: 2

Ingredients:

*   90 grams all-purpose flour
*   Pinch of salt
*   1/2 teaspoon of baking powder
*   ½ cup of tutti fruitti mix
*   2 eggs
*   1 teaspoon of vanilla extract
*   10 tablespoons of white sugar

Preparation:

1. Take a bowl and add all-purpose flour, salt, and baking powder.
2. Stir it in a large bowl.
3. Whisk two eggs in a separate bowl and add vanilla extract, sugar and blend it with a hand beater.
4. Now combine wet ingredients with the dry ones.
5. Mix it well and pour it into round pan that fits inside basket.
6. Place the pan inside the basket.
7. Now set it to BAKE function at 310 for 30 minutes.
8. Once it's done, serve and enjoy.

Serving Suggestion: Serve it with whipped cream

Variation Tip: Use brown sugar instead of white sugar

Nutritional Information Per Serving:

Calories 711| Fat 4.8g| Sodium 143mg | Carbs 161g | Fiber 1.3g | Sugar 105g | Protein 10.2g

Bread Pudding

Prep Time: 12 minutes.

Cook Time: 8-12 minutes.

Serves: 2

Ingredients:

*   Nonstick spray, for greasing ramekins
*   2 slices of white bread, crumbled
*   4 tablespoons of white sugar
*   5 large eggs

- ½ cup cream
- Salt, pinch
- 1/3 teaspoon of cinnamon powder

Preparation:

1. Take a bowl and whisk eggs in it.
2. Add sugar and salt to the egg and whisk it all well.
3. Then add cream and use a hand beater to incorporate the entire ingredients.
4. Now add cinnamon, and add crumbs of bread.
5. Mix it well and add into a round shaped baking pan.
6. Put it inside the ninja air fryer.
7. Set it on AIRFRY mode at 350 degrees F for 8-12 minutes.
8. Once it's cooked, serve.

Serving Suggestion: Serve it with Coffee

Variation Tip: Use brown sugar instead of white sugar

Nutritional Information Per Serving:

Calories 331| Fat 16.1g| Sodium 331mg| Carbs 31g| Fiber 0.2g | Sugar 26.2g | Protein 16.2g

Air Fryer Sweet Twists

Prep Time: 15 minutes.

Cook Time: 10 minutes.

Serves: 2

Ingredients:

- 1 box store-bought puff pastry
- ½ teaspoon cinnamon
- ½ teaspoon sugar
- ½ teaspoon black sesame seeds
- Salt, pinch
- 2 tablespoons Parmesan cheese, freshly grated

Preparation:

1. Place the dough on a work surface.
2. Take a small bowl and mix cheese, sugar, salt, sesame seeds, and cinnamon.
3. Press this mixture on both sides of the dough.
4. Now, cut the pastry into 1" x 3" strips.
5. Twist each of the strips 2 times and then lay it onto the flat.
6. Transfer it to the air fryer basket.

7. Select the air fry mode at 400 degrees F for 10 minutes.
8. Once cooked, serve.

Serving Suggestion: Serve it with champagne!

Variation Tip: None

Nutritional Information Per Serving:

Calories 140| Fat 9.4g| Sodium 142mg| Carbs 12.3g| Fiber 0.8 g | Sugar 1.2g | Protein 2g

Pumpkin Muffins

Prep Time: 20 minutes.

Cook Time: 19 minutes.

Serves: 4

Ingredients:

- 1 and ½ cups of all-purpose flour
- ½ teaspoon baking soda
- ½ teaspoon of baking powder
- 1 and 1/4 teaspoons cinnamon, groaned
- 1/4 teaspoon ground nutmeg, grated
- 2 large eggs
- Salt, pinch
- 3/4 cup granulated sugar
- 1/2 cup dark brown sugar
- 1 and 1/2 cups of pumpkin puree
- 1/4 cup coconut milk

Preparation:

1. Take 4 ramekins that are the size of a cup and layer them with muffin papers.
2. Crack an egg in a bowl and add brown sugar, baking soda, baking powder, cinnamon, nutmeg, and sugar.
3. Whisk it all very well with an electric hand beater.
4. Now, in a second bowl, mix the flour, and salt.
5. Now, mix the dry ingredients slowly with the wet ingredients.
6. Now, at the end fold in the pumpkin puree and milk, mix it well
7. Divide this batter into 4 ramekins.
8. Now, put the ramekins inside the basket.
9. Add basket to the unit.
10. Set the time to 18 minutes at 360 degrees Fat AIRFRY mode.
11. Check if not done, and let it AIR FRY for one more minute.
12. Once it is done, serve.

Serving Suggestion: Serve it with a glass of milk

Variation Tip: Use almond milk instead of coconut milk

Nutritional Information Per Serving:

Calories 291| Fat 6.4 g| Sodium 241mg | Carbs 57.1g | Fiber 4.4g | Sugar 42g | Protein 5.9g

Lemony Sweet Twists

Prep Time: 15 minutes.

Cook Time: 9 minutes.

Serves: 2

Ingredients:

- 1 box store-bought puff pastry
- ½ teaspoon lemon zest
- 1 tablespoon of lemon juice
- 2 teaspoons brown sugar
- Salt, pinch
- 2 tablespoons Parmesan cheese, freshly grated

Preparation:

1. Put the puff pastry dough on a clean work area.
2. In a bowl, combine Parmesan cheese, brown sugar, salt, lemon zest, and lemon juice.
3. Press this mixture on both sides of the dough.
4. Now, cut the pastry into 1" x 4" strips.
5. Twist each of the strips.
6. Transfer it to the air fryer basket.
7. Select the air fry mode at 400 degrees F for 9-10 minutes.
8. Once cooked, serve and enjoy.

Serving Suggestion: Serve it with champagne!

Variation Tip: None

Nutritional Information Per Serving:

Calories 156| Fat 10g| Sodium 215mg | Carbs 14g | Fiber 0.4g | Sugar 3.3 g | Protein 2.8g

Fudge Brownies

Prep Time: 20 minutes.

Cook Time: 35 minutes.

Serves: 4

Ingredients:

- 1/2 cup all-purpose flour
- 1/4 cup unsweetened cocoa powder
- 3/4 teaspoon kosher salt
- 2 large eggs, whisked
- 1 tablespoon almond milk
- 1/2 cup brown sugar
- 1/2 cup packed white sugar
- 1/2 tablespoon vanilla extract
- 8 ounces of semisweet chocolate chips, melted
- 2/4 cup unsalted butter, melted

Preparation:

1. Take a medium bowl, and use a hand beater to whisk together eggs, milk, both the sugars and vanilla.
2. In a separate microwave-safe bowl, mix melted butter and chocolate and microwave it for 30 seconds to melt the chocolate.
3. Add all the listed dry ingredients to the chocolate mixture.
4. Now incorporate the egg bowl ingredient into the batter.
5. Spray a reasonable size round baking pan that fits in basket of air fryer.
6. Grease the pan with cooking spray.
7. Now pour the batter into the pan, put the crisper plate in basket.
8. Add the pan and insert the basket into the unit.
9. Select the AIR FRY mode and adjust the setting the temperature to 300 degrees F, for 30 minutes.
10. Check it after 35 minutes and if not done, cook for 10 more minutes
11. Once it's done, take it out and let it get cool before serving.
12. Enjoy.

Serving Suggestion: Serve it with a dollar of the vanilla ice cream

Variation Tip: Use dairy milk instead of almond milk

Nutritional Information Per Serving:

Calories 760| Fat 43.3g| Sodium 644mg| Carbs 93.2g| Fiber 5.3g| Sugar 70.2g| Protein 6.2g

Chocolate Chip Muffins

Prep Time: 12 minutes.

Cook Time: 15 minutes.

Serves: 2

Ingredients:

- Salt, pinch
- 2 eggs
- 1/3 cup brown sugar
- 1/3 cup butter
- 4 tablespoons of milk
- ¼ teaspoon of vanilla extract
- ½ teaspoon of baking powder
- 1 cup all-purpose flour
- 1 pouch chocolate chips, 35 grams

Preparation:

1.   Take 4 oven-safe ramekins that are the size of a cup and layer them with muffin papers.

2.   In a bowl, whisk the egg, brown sugar, butter, milk, and vanilla extract.

3.   Whisk it all very well with an electric hand beater.

4.   Now, in a second bowl, mix the flour, baking powder, and salt.

5.   Now, mix the dry ingredients slowly into the wet ingredients.

6.   Now, at the end fold in the chocolate chips and mix them well

7.   Divide this batter into 4 ramekins.

8.   Now, put the ramekins in the basket.

9.   Set the time to 15 minutes at 350 degrees F, at AIRFRY mode.

10. Check if not done, and let it AIR FRY for one more minute.

11. Once it is done, serve.

Serving Suggestion: Serve it with chocolate syrup drizzle

Variation Tip: None

Nutritional Information Per Serving:

Calories 757| Fat 40.3g| Sodium 426mg| Carbs 85.4g| Fiber 2.2g| Sugar 30.4g| Protein 14.4g

Chocolate Chip Cake

Prep Time: 12 minutes.

Cook Time: 15 minutes.

Serves: 4

Ingredients:

- Salt, pinch
- 2 eggs, whisked
- ½ cup brown sugar
- ½ cup butter, melted
- 10 tablespoons of almond milk
- ¼ teaspoon of vanilla extract
- ½ teaspoon of baking powder
- 1 cup all-purpose flour
- 1 cup of chocolate chips
- ½ cup of cocoa powder

Preparation:

1. Take a large baking pan that fits inside the basket of the air fryer.
2. Layer it with baking paper, cut it to the size of a baking pan.
3. In a bowl, whisk the egg, brown sugar, butter, almond milk, and vanilla extract.
4. Whisk it all very well with an electric hand beater.
5. In a second bowl, mix the flour, cocoa powder, baking powder, and salt.
6. Now, mix the dry ingredients slowly with the wet ingredients.
7. Now, at the end fold in the chocolate chips.
8. Incorporate all the ingredients well.
9. Pour this batter into the round baking pan.
10. put it inside the basket.
11. Set the time to 15 minutes at 350 degrees F at AIR FRY mode.
12. Check if not done, and let it AIR FRY for one more minute.
13. Once it is done, serve.

Serving Suggestion: Serve it with chocolate syrup drizzle

Variation Tip: Use baking soda instead of baking powder

Nutritional Information Per Serving:

Calories 736| Fat 45.5g| Sodium 356mg| Carbs 78.2g| Fiber 6.1g| Sugar 32.7g| Protein11.5 g

Mini Blueberry Pies

Prep Time: 12 minutes.

Cook Time: 10 minutes.

Serves: 2

Ingredients:

•   1 box Store-Bought Pie Dough, Trader Joe's

•   ¼ cup blueberry jam

•   1 teaspoon of lemon zest

•   1 egg white, for brushing

Preparation:

1.   Take the store brought pie dough and cut it into 3-inch circles.

2.   Brush the dough with egg white all around the parameters.

3.   Now add blueberry jam and zest in the middle and top it with another circular.

4.   Press the edges with the fork to seal it.

5.   Make a slit in the middle of the dough and transfer it to the basket.

6.   Set it to AIR FRY mode at 360 degrees for 10 minutes.

7.   Once cooked, serve.

Serving Suggestion: Serve it with vanilla ice-cream

Variation Tip: use orange zest instead of lemon zest

Nutritional Information Per Serving:

Calories 234| Fat 8.6g| Sodium 187mg| Carbs 38.2g| Fiber 0.1g| Sugar 13.7g| Protein 2g

Mini Strawberry and Cream Pies

Prep Time: 12 minutes.

Cook Time: 10 minutes.

Serves: 2

Ingredients:

•   1 box Store-Bought Pie Dough, Trader Joe's

•   1 cup strawberries, cubed

•   3 tablespoons of cream, heavy

•   2 tablespoons of almonds

•   1 egg white, for brushing

Preparation:

1.   Take the store brought pie dough and flatten it on a surface.

2.   Use a round cutter to cut it into 3-inch circles.

3.   Brush the dough with egg white all around the parameters.

4.   Now add almonds, strawberries, and cream in a very little amount in the center of the dough, and top it with another circular.

5.   Press the edges with the fork to seal it.

6.   Make a slit in the middle of the dough and put it into the basket.

7.   Set it to AIR FRY mode 360 degrees for 10 minutes.

8.   Once done, serve.

Serving Suggestion: Serve it with vanilla ice-cream

Variation Tip: use orange zest instead of lemon zest

Nutritional Information Per Serving:

Calories 203| Fat 12.7g| Sodium 193mg | Carbs 20g | Fiber 2.2g | Sugar 5.8g | Protein 3.7g

Conclusion

A smart Air Fryer has become the need of today. Gone are the days when people could rely on deep oil frying; as we are living in the age of tech-smart kitchen appliances now, Air frying can offer the same results without the use of excess oil. The Air frying cooking technique is much healthier and cooks crispy food every time with low-fat content. Ninja food tech company has therefore launched its own series of Air Fryers, which can offer even frying at any temperature. The shape of the appliance gives it an extra edge over the other competing models in the market, as it has a broad base containing sufficient space inside its cooking basket. To make the device more versatile in its function, it comes with manually controlled temperature and timing operations, whereas there are also other modes of cooking available that provide preset settings. This Ninja Air fryer cookbook is designed to highlight several of its other amazing features while providing a range of recipes that can be cooked using this Air fryer. If you are always in the mood to enjoy some crisp, then Ninja Air fryer is all for you, and this cookbook can be your ultimate guide.

By looking at the control panel of the ninja Air fryer, you will realize how simple and user-friendly its mechanism is. You don't need to constantly check and set the hardware or the software. Just plug it in and select the desired mode, time, and temperature, and press start. By its single-button technology, it gives easier access to all of its users. The preset modes allow even easier handling of the device. The assembly of all of its accessories, from the Air Fryer Basket to the crisper plate and the rack, is also quite simple. Follow the steps discussed above, and anyone can become the Ninja Air fryer expert. It takes just 2 to 3 sessions of cooking with the device to fully understand its control. The Ninja Air fryer is not completely an Air fryer like other companies offer in the market. Besides the Air frying mode, it also offers other modes of cooking, including the roasting mode, the reheating, and dehydrating mode. The cooking techniques used in this device are also appropriate for roasting food and dehydrating it. So, let's get started with some smart oil-free cooking!

Made in the USA
Coppell, TX
07 May 2021